WRESTLING
HEROES & VILLAINS

BEEKMAN HOUSE
New York

INTRODUCTION

ISBN: 0-517-48933-3

This edition published by:
Beekman House
Distributed by
Crown Publishers, Inc.
One Park Avenue
New York, New York 10016

Manufactured in the United States of America
10 9 8 7 6 5 4 3 2 1

Written by: George J. Napolitano
Editorial assistance and research: Jacqueline Quartarano, Jeremy Tepper, Jim Schuermann, Mike Allen, Mike Edison, and Phyliss Pucket.

Cover photos: Walter Iooss, Jr., William Hart, George Napolitano

Back cover: Walter Iooss, Jr.

Photo Credits: Box Photo, pp. 88, 90; Stephen Crichlow, p. 88; Peter Dinger, pp. 16, 54; Globe Photos, pp. 20, 22, 23, 25, 26, 52, 53, 92, 93, 95; Globe Photos/Adam Scull, pp. 27, 66; William Hart, pp. 7, 24, 25, 34, 45, 55, 78, 81; Walter Iooss, Jr., pp. 40, 64, 65, 67, 73, 76, 77, 79, 80; George Napolitano, pp. 4, 5, 8, 9, 11, 12, 13, 14, 15, 17, 18, 19, 21, 28, 29, 30, 32, 33, 35, 36, 37, 38, 39, 40, 42, 43, 44, 46, 49, 51, 58, 59, 60, 61, 62, 63, 66, 69, 71, 74, 75, 83, 84, 85, 86, 87, 89, 91; Personality Photos Inc./Titan Sports Inc. (WWF), pp. 6, 31, 47, 50, 56, 57; Personality Photos Inc./Steve Taylor (Titan Sports Inc.; WWF), p. 94; Wide World Photos, pp. 25, 96

Wrestling has been a part of our culture from the dawn of time. In fact, it was one of the first Olympic sports. Today, people don't equate Olympic wrestling competition with the professional variety, but there is a very obvious connection: Many of today's professional stars began in the amateur ranks.

College wrestling is considered by many to be dull and boring, but nobody could level that criticism at the professional variety. Call it a sport, call it entertainment, call it anything you want, but the bottom line is that over 25 million people attended wrestling bouts last year. Diehard aficionados have always gone wild over the sport, but now the whole world seems to have contracted wrestling mania. Professional wrestling has literally exploded.

Four of the top ten cable TV shows are wrestling programs, and one network has taken a flying leap into the ring with the inaugural telecast of NBC-TV's "Saturday Night's Main Event" special. Wrestlers are showing up in all kinds of entertainment-related settings outside of the wrestling ring. For instance, in toy stores across the land you can now find dolls representing grapplers like Hulk Hogan, Andre the Giant, and Big John Studd. The Hulkster and Andre will also be the stars of a new CBS-TV animated cartoon to be shown on Saturday mornings.

Captain Lou Albano, a former wrestler who is now a manager, played Cyndi Lauper's father in the music video of "Girls Just Want To Have Fun," and will have a role in Brian De Palma's new comedy, *Wiseguys*; he plays a Mafia hit man named Frankie the Fixer.

Wrestling night in New York's Madison Square Garden has become a happening. You might rub elbows with Diane Keaton, Andy Warhol, Danny DeVito, Joe Piscopo, or Brian De Palma. You might find yourself cheering along with Cyndi Lauper, Billy Squier, or Twisted Sister. Wrestling fans have come out of the closet: Professional wrestling is now chic. It's become the thing to do to talk about the exploits of the Iron Sheik, Roddy Piper's unsavory interviews, and the conquests of the Hulkster.

Many fans who have recently rediscovered professional wrestling remember the sport as it was in their youth. They have vivid recollections of the high-flying maneuvers of Antonino Rocca, the antics of Nature Boy Buddy Rogers, the unpredictable moves of Dick the Bruiser, the incredible strength of Bruno Sammartino. They recall Chief Jay Strongbow's war dance and the dastardly deeds of Professor Tanaka. Whenever the subject of wrestling comes up, you'll hear someone say, "Whatever happened to...?"

As it happens, the new-found wrestling mania is not new at all. Since 1963, when Bruno Sammartino won the WWF Heavyweight Title from Buddy Rogers, a ticket for the wrestling bouts has been the hottest ticket in town. In the past 20 years there have been no more than a dozen times when the Garden did not sell out. Yet the media and the press now proclaim the wrestling craze a new phenomenom. Today's "new" fans have been following the sport for years; they just didn't talk about it because being a fan of wrestling wasn't considered chic. Now they're turning out in droves to cheer the heroes and jeer the villains.

The stars of the sport cross all geographic boundaries. Due to the proliferation of cable TV stations, you can sit comfortably at home and can watch stars from around the globe in combat. Hulk Hogan is as popular in New York as he is in California; Kerry Von Erich has as many fans in Boston as he has in Dallas; the Iron Sheik is as despised in Washington, D.C. as he is in Toronto, Canada. Professional wrestling is regional, national, and international all at once, and, of course, the stars of the sport are the common attraction that keeps record numbers of fans all over the world pouring through the turnstiles or glued to their TVs.

This book is a celebration of today's professional wrestling, profiling in words and pictures the most admired heroes and the most despised villains. Welcome to the wild, wild world of professional wrestling.

CONTENTS

HEROES   VILLAINS   TAG TEAMS   WOMEN

Use the color coding system at left to determine whether a wrestler is a hero, a villain, a tag team member, or a woman.

ANDRE THE GIANT

Weight: 497 pounds
Hometown: Grenoble, France
Best Move: The Body Slam
Titles Held: None

He's known as the "Eighth Wonder of the World," and the 7'5", 497-pound Giant from Grenoble, France, is indeed the greatest sports attraction in the world today.

They don't come any tougher than Andre the Giant. They certainly don't come any bigger, and it is his immense stature that has enabled Andre to become the top box-office attraction in wrestling. Despite his weight and size, Andre moves like a man half his size. He has a sound fundamental approach to the sport but once angered, Andre can get as wild as any of today's top rulebreakers.

Just ask Killer Kahn his opinion of Andre! Kahn still shudders at the mere mention of Andre's name. It must be noted, however, that Kahn is the only man ever to seriously injure the Giant. The injury occured during a match in Boston after Kahn knocked Andre to the mat. The Mongolian mounted the ring ropes and then came crashing down from the third rope, breaking Andre's leg in two places.

Andre spent the next two weeks in the hospital and then had to hobble around on crutches for two more weeks. You just had to know that someday Andre would get his sweet revenge on Kahn—and he did! After Andre got through with Kahn, the Mongolian madman took the next plane headed to "Outer Mongolia" and never returned to the WWF.

Although Andre's bout with Kahn was his most celebrated, Andre has had several other major battles. The Giant's first major encounter occured in 1971 against the 6'8" Mormon Don Leo Jonathan. For close to a year, these two battled all over Canada.

Andre the Giant (left) is one of the biggest, if not the biggest, men in wrestling today. His towering height and massive bulk give him a built-in advantage against smaller competitors. Just look at how he handles Redneck Murdoch (right).

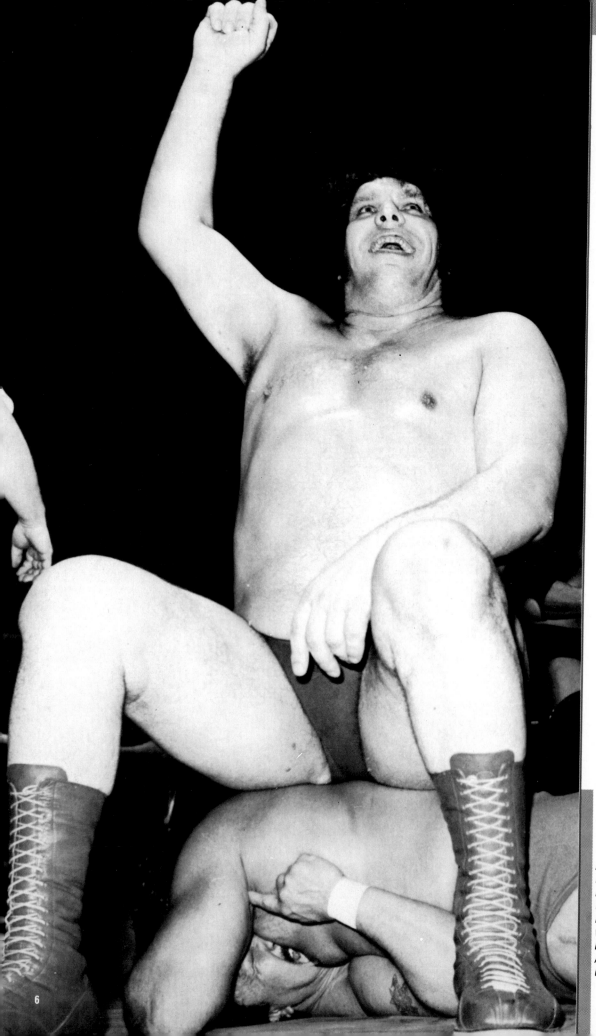

Finally, Andre defeated his rival in the Montreal Forum, proving once and for all that he was indeed a major star. After his series of bouts against Jonathan, Andre headed to the United States.

In any given week, Andre may be seen wrestling in Miami, Dallas, Los Angeles, Minneapolis, New York, Montreal, and Tokyo—the Giant rarely if ever has a day off. Although it's a tough grind, Andre loves his life. "Wrestling has been good to me," Andre has stated. "I've been able to tour the world, meet friends all over the globe, and just live life to its fullest."

Although the Giant has battled the biggest and best men in the profession, he has nothing but praise and admiration for his opponents—everyone, that is, except Big John Studd. For the past two years, Studd and Andre have been waging a personal war all over the world. Studd simply can't accept the idea that there is someone bigger and tougher than he.

Studd and Andre have battled on numerous occasions and each battle has been a fight to the finish. Not too long ago, Studd, along with Bobby Heenan and Ken Patera, cut off Andre's hair. The trio then went around bragging about their accomplishment.

It took him some time, but Andre has now gotten back at the devious threesome. The first to feel Andre's wrath was Ken Patera, whom Andre flattened in a bout in Madison Square Garden. At the big WrestleMania extravaganza, Andre won $15,000 when he body slammed the big man to the mat.

What's next for the Giant? Anything that he wants. Andre literally has the world at his feet and whatever goals the Giant has in mind, no one can stop him from attaining.

A triumphant Andre totally humiliates his opponent (left). Despite his fierce looks and threatening size, he's a cheerful man who respects all his fellow wrestlers. Everyone, that is, but Big John Studd, the man who cut Andre's hair while the Giant was unconscious in the ring.

ABDULLAH
THE BUTCHER

Weight: 360 pounds
Hometown: The Sudan
Best Move: Using Foreign Objects
Titles Held: WWC Carribean
  Champion

You won't see a display of wrestling skills when Abdullah the Butcher enters the ring. The Suplexes, Leglocks, Sunset Flips, and Armdrags will all be left in the locker room when it's Abdullah's turn to wrestle. At 360 pounds, you cannot Suplex him. You cannot Piledrive him. All you will see is blood. His maniacal bloodlust will turn any wrestling match into a horror show. After all, he isn't called "The Butcher" for nothing.

Abdullah was born into the Eleventh Tribe of Sudan. As a young man there, he was required to kill desert cows with his bare hands to prove his manhood. The animal would then be slaughtered and the blood drunk in the belief that it would bring prosperity and wealth. Thus began Abdullah's unquenchable thirst.

It is generally believed that Abdullah was exiled from his tribe because his desire to maim and kill erupted into several incidents with fellow tribesmen. He was put on a slow ship to the Carribean, the islands where Abdullah embarked on his new career—wrestling.

Abdullah's style of wrestling is devoid of agility and scientific skill in the traditional sense—to see him gouge an eye or tear open an opponent is to see a true mayhem artist in action. Soon promoters discovered that his awe-inspiring presence and penchant for blood was a guaranteed success at the box office. Abdullah began wrestling for the World Wrestling Council in San Juan, where he quickly became the WWC

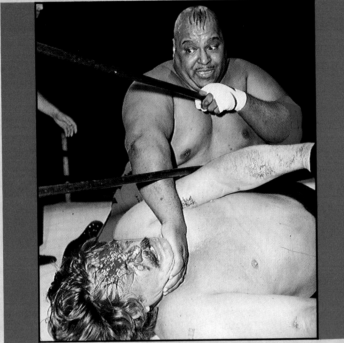

When Abdullah the Butcher steps into the ring, blood has a curious tendency to flow.

Carribean Champ and the number one contender for the prestigious Universal Title, which was then held by Carlos Colon.

"*Mira! Mira!* Look at my head!" hollered Carlos, pointing to his heavily scarred forehead. And then very slowly, with more than a tinge of fear—like a man who has seen death—he whispered "Abdullah." It's a fitting testimony to a butcher who might just as well have carved his name in Colon's head. With a pallet of forks, butcher knives, and razors, the Butcher turned the Universal Champ's forehead into an ugly mass of scar tissue. There was never any chance for the talented champion to baffle the heathen Abdullah with science or his superior athletic ability. There was only a slim chance of not losing

too much blood.

Abdullah's reputation as "Master of the Foreign Object" spread to nearby Florida, where he started another blood-soaked feud with a man almost his equal in stature, Dusty Rhodes. These awe-inspiring matches were blood baths of the first order. Fans watched in fear as these titans went at it with barbecue forks in steel cages. Fans saw Abdullah bust himself open with the timekeeper's bell and hungrily lap up his own blood. They witnessed Abdullah ripping a three-inch chunk of flesh from Dusty's arm. And then finally, they saw these men go at it in a barbed-wire fence match. This time, Abdullah and his promoters went too far, and Florida has never been the same.

A barbed-wire fence match is the most dangerous type of wrestling match there is. It's like having a license to maim, disfigure, and perhaps even *kill* your opponent. But Abdullah was quite at home in a ring surrounded with deadly razor ribbon. While Dusty screamed in agony, Abdullah delighted in the insane battle like a child on Christmas morning. These two men ripped each other to gory shreds. Many fans fainted and those at ringside were splattered with blood and torn flesh. Finally, the match was stopped and Dusty was helped from the ring. Abdullah the Butcher stuck around to lap up some blood and display a sickening grin.

Abdullah's name became synonymous throughout the world with mayhem. Many desperate wrestlers tried to enlist him as a mercenary, only to discover that his bloodlust outweighs any concept of loyalty. There is no trying to control or manage him, for he is a savage.

Abdullah moved to the AWA for a short time where he carved up the likes of Tommy Rich, Blackjack Mulligan, and Crusher Blackwell.

Even with his lack of any conventional wrestling knowledge, Abdullah the Butcher has proven to be one of the most dangerous men in the sport. One can only wonder what might happen if Abdullah were to go after the World Championship.

Abdullah the Butcher is not a wrestler—he's a walking blood bath. An unabashed cannibal, he eagerly tears apart human flesh and drinks human blood—even his own!

JERRY "CRUSHER" BLACKWELL

Weight: 468 pounds
Hometown: Stone Mountain, Georgia
Best Move: The Big Splash
Titles Held: AWA World Tag Team Champion (with Ken Patera)

Professional wrestling contains many big men who hold significant weight advantages over their smaller opponents. Such a big man is Jerry "Crusher" Blackwell, who stands 6'2" and weighs in at an incredible 468 pounds! With dimensions such as these, it is easy to see why the big man from Stone Mountain, Georgia, hovers over many of wrestling's medium-sized competitors.

Looking at Blackwell, most people would think he is slow, clumsy, and out of shape. This could not be further from the truth, because Blackwell is one of the best athletes in wrestling today. One of his favorite moves is performing a Flying Drop Kick from six feet in the air onto an opponent's jaw, a maneuver usually reserved for men much lighter than he. The Crusher can also move around the ring with the speed of a light heavyweight, tossing his opponents from post to post as he softens them up for one of his patented Big Splashes. The moment the Crusher lands on his poor opponent, the referee has no choice but to count to three and chalk up another impressive victory for Blackwell.

When he first entered the AWA six years ago, Blackwell was one of the most hated men in the arena. His sadistic streak and wicked ways drove him to the top of the rankings and finally, a shot at the title held by Verne Gagne. Their matches were wild, and it

was only after a long, hard battle that Gagne finally disposed of the Crusher.

After failing to win the AWA Heavyweight championship, Blackwell became the protégé of Sheik Adnan El'Kaissey. The Sheik had hoped to win the AWA World Tag Team title from Greg Gagne and Jim Brunzell, but unfortunately his plans were nixed when the Sheik had his arm broken by Mad Dog Vachon and Verne Gagne in an especially ferocious match. With his arm in a cast and his pride cut to shreds, the Sheik purchased Ken Patera's contract from Bobby Heenan for $500,000 and molded Blackwell and Patera into one of the meanest teams in wrestling.

The Sheik's investment paid off immediately, with Blackwell and Patera capturing the tag belts and holding on to them for almost one year until they were upset by another wrestler named the Crusher and Baron Von Raschke. After losing the titles, the Sheik flew into a tirade, vowing to punish all of his many enemies for causing his men to lose the titles. Intent on revenge, the Sheik brought King Kong Brody and Abdullah the Butcher to the AWA, and the two wildmen created nothing but mayhem and violence in the ring.

Both paid assassins carried out their mission according to plan as they kicked, scratched, and bloodied everyone they met in the ring. After it seemed that their mission was complete, the Sheik surprised the world by instructing Brody and the Butcher to attack Crusher Blackwell. Their savage attack left Blackwell unconscious and bleeding profusely in the center of the ring. After being rushed to a nearby hospital,

Blackwell quietly left the AWA and returned to Georgia to ponder his next move.

Following a two-month, self-imposed exile, Blackwell returned to the scene of the crime with one goal in mind: To settle the score with the Sheik. In order to reach the Sheik, Blackwell first had to battle his army of mercenaries, which included Brody, Mr. Saito, "Crazy" Luke Graham, King Tonga, and Masked Superstar. Unfazed by such an impossible task, Blackwell set out to destroy the Sheik's band of men one by one until he could finally get Adnan in the ring. But unfortunately, the match never occurred, since the Sheik always hid behind his wrestlers, refusing to get into the ring with "that big, fat slob."

Blackwell's return immediately made him the most popular man in the ring—a direct contrast from his early days when he was the most hated villain. Even though he was now a favorite, Blackwell remained a brutal, sadistic wrestler who delighted in dishing out punishment to his opponents. The only difference was that now he was on the side of law and order, and not on the side of the Sheik.

When it was apparent that Blackwell could not stop the Sheik all by himself, he enlisted the aid of the all-American hero, Sergeant Slaughter. In no time, Slaughter and Blackwell formed a devastating tag team and they have battled the Sheik and his men in some of the most violent matches in AWA history.

The animosity between Blackwell and the Sheik soon deepened from a personal vendetta into a battle of national pride. The final chapter of their

long, bitter feud came when the men met in a no-holds-barred steel cage match. After nearly 20 minutes of nonstop brutality, the team of Slaughter and Blackwell came out victorious, thus ending the spree of senseless violence engineered by the bloodthirsty Sheik.

After such a violent battle, most people would sit back and rest on their laurels, but not Jerry Blackwell. He has continued his tag team effort with Slaughter and now has his sights set on the Road Warriors and the belts which he once proudly controlled. Given his formula of hard work, dedication, and his ability to take punishment, it may only be a matter of time before Blackwell once again sits at the top of the tag team hill.

Crusher Blackwell wrestled for Sheik Adnan El'Kaissey until the Sheik turned Abdullah the Butcher and King Kong Brody loose on Blackwell. Betrayed, Crusher joined forces with Sgt. Slaughter and settled the score.

RIC FLAIR

Weight: 240 pounds
Hometown: Minneapolis, Minnesota
Best Move: The Figure-Four Leglock
Titles Held: Missouri Heavyweight Champion, U.S. Heavyweight Champion, NWA World Heavyweight Champion

The only true World's Champion stands in the studio, adjusting his sunglasses and tightening his grip on the most coveted belt in wrestling. "When you look at me," Ric Flair barks, "you're looking at the finest that wrestling has to offer. I set the standard!" This is no idle boast. Ric Flair is a champion for the '80s, the holder of the most prestigious title in wrestling—the NWA World's Heavyweight Championship.

Flair has been one of grappling's most gifted competitors since he debuted in the early '70s. He won both the Missouri and U.S. titles at an early age, burning through his opponents like propane gas.

Although his arrogance is deplored by most fans, insiders and fanatics marvel at his command of the language of wrestling. It is as if the collective wisdom of all wrestlers dating back to antiquity has been passed on to Flair.

Since he whupped Dusty Rhodes for the NWA World's Title in 1981, Flair has guarded the ten pounds of gold with the jealousy of a miser. His body has undergone horrendous suffering in the defense of his belt. A backbreaking schedule has taken its toll, but it also has intensified his desire to hang on to the title. Flair himself revealed the depth of his sense of duty when he said, "If being the U.S. Champion was like serving in the U.S. Senate, then being World Champion is like being the President. There is a whole new set of responsibilities."

Flair is currently well into a third championship reign, and it is the way he regained his title twice that proves his dominance in the sport. It took him little more than five months to thrash out a bloody ransom from Harley Race in 1983, and he merely loaned the title to Kerry Von Erich for three weeks the following year. Neither Race nor Von Erich could make the title their own before Ric Flair tapped on the window and demanded his due.

What is it that makes Ric Flair the people's champion? One could begin with a comparison of Flair and the two other world champs, AWA titlist Rick Martel and WWF kingpin Hulk Hogan. Martel is a talented young grappler, but his attack is plodding and workmanlike compared to Flair's, and he lacks Ric's experience and aggressiveness. Hogan has never wrestled a one-hour time-limit draw, and his repertoire of maneuvers is so severely limited that he'd be a pushover for Flair.

Another thing that makes Ric Flair the Cadillac of champions is his independence. The vast majority of wrestlers waste time and energy either courting the fans or abusing them. Ric Flair was strictly a "bag guy" at the outset of his career, but the championship has changed him. He is determined to avoid the kind of feuds that distract other wrestlers. A Ric Flair title match is virtually never the culmination of some senseless struggle with a fan favorite or rulebreaker. For men like Dusty Rhodes and Sgt. Slaughter, or Kevin Sullivan and Abdullah the Butcher, wrestling is a brutal crusade to defend the forces of light or darkness. Ric Flair is not a metaphysical wrestler; he wants to win simply to prove he is the best man.

The most controversial aspect of Flair's career has been his lifestyle. He's bonkers for the good life. He takes pride in maintaining a rigorous social calendar, and brags about the thousands of women who have felt his caresses. Most athletes could not survive Flair's party pace and still stick to their training regimen, but Ric is a dynamo. He requires very little sleep, and, at this point, very little training; wrestling comes naturally to him. Most importantly, there is no grappler in the game with less need of a manager than Ric Flair, since his personal library of up-to-date scouting reports is more extensive than those of many managerial stables.

Nonetheless, the primary criticism of Flair throughout his career has been that he doesn't "conduct himself like a champion." Many wrestling fans and insiders prefer the traditional image of a champion as a family man who turns in after the ten o'clock news and sets a good example for the kids. Flair will never be the clean-cut champion that men like Bob Backlund or Bruno Sammartino were, but attitudes must change in wrestling as they have in other sports. Ric Flair may lead a decadent lifestyle, but he never leaves his fight in the nightclub.

Technically, Flair is any man's equal in the ring. His specialty is the dreaded Figure-Four Leglock, which he applies with enough symmetry and force to snap tree trunks. Lesser wrestlers assume that their Figure-Four, once applied, is just as painful as any other, and don't bother to execute the hold with precision. But Flair's is superior for a number of reasons. He slaps it on as quickly as any man, which is crucial since a split-second pause in the middle can result in kicks and punches from the hapless victim. (Greg Valentine, whose Figure-Four could be the most *powerful* in wrestling, is considerably

slower in application and suffers for it.) Flair also likes to sit up and face his agonized opponent once the hold is applied. A straight-ahead Figure-Four is more difficult to reverse, since it deprives the opponent of leverage to twist out. Flair's Figure-Four Leglock is peerless; the only others comparable belong to Carlos Colon, Dusty Rhodes (because of the bulk of his legs), the now semi-retired Pat Patterson, and Greg Valentine.

The Figure-Four Leglock is just part of Flair's arsenal of pain. Actually, he rarely concentrates on the limbs to weaken an opponent, preferring to utilize his incredible upper-body strength. His Suplexes are devastating, and Flair has mastered them all. He is also particularly dangerous when groping for an advantage on the mat, where his prolific scientific skills come into play. Flair can pin you with scientific trickery just as easily as with a thundering Double-Underhook Suplex.

Ric Flair began his career as a charter member of the Buddy Rogers Admiration Society, consciously imitating the only man to win both the NWA and WWF world titles by calling himself "Nature Boy," and specializing in the Figure-Four. As Flair improved, though, comparisons became superfluous, and it became obvious that they shared only one attribute in common—greatness. Today, Flair has his own imitators. Great young grapplers like Tully Blanchard (who has the potential to someday be Flair's equal) and well-meaning nobodies like Buddy Landell (whose slavish emulation—he too calls himself "Nature Boy"—brings to mind Elvis impersonators) have copped Flair's style and technique. Young wrestlers who go up against Flair discuss it afterwards in terms of an educational experience rather than just a beating.

Ric Flair uses his prodigious wrestling talents against his opponent, Gino Hernandez. Flair has dominated the NWA World's Title since 1981, enduring great hardship to keep the belt.

CARLOS COLON

Weight: 225 pounds
Hometown: San Isabela, Puerto Rico
Best Move: The Somersault Leap
Titles Held: Universal Champion, WWC Heavyweight Champion

Carlos Colon first learned the basic of the sport in a wrestling school run by the late, great Antonino Rocca. From the moment young Colon walked into the gym and saw the legendary Rocca giving pointers to the youngsters, he was hooked. Two years later, Colon turned professional and he's been on the road ever since. "Wrestling is the best thing that ever happened to me," the talented Colon admitted. "It's enabled me to travel around the world and experience things that I never would have been able to had I not gone into the sport."

During his career, the high flying Colon has won numerous titles. The two he is most proud of are the WWC Heavyweight belt and the Universal championship. To win the WWC belt, Colon had to defeat his arch-rival Abdullah the Butcher. The bout was held in front of a standing-room-only crowd in the Roberto Clemente Coliseum in San Juan, Puerto Rico, in August 1982. The moment Abdullah entered the ring swinging the championship belt in his hand, Colon knew that it would be a fight for survival. During the bout, Colon took everything Abdullah had to offer while dishing out his own medicine. Finally, after 15 minutes of pure mayhem, Abdullah was knocked out cold. All that was left for Colon was to pounce on his rival for the victory and the championship.

As champion, Colon put his

The indomitable Carlos Colon inflicts a Neckbreaker on his tired, helpless victim.

title on the line against a formidable line-up containing the who's who of wrestling. His challengers included such stars as Dory Funk, Jr., Terry Funk, Bobby Jaggers, King Kong Mosca, King Tonga, and even Roddy Piper. They all tried to ply the belt away from the champion, but no one succeeded. "I've never backed down from my challenge," Colon admitted. "If someone thinks they can defeat me, the only thing they have to do is sign their name on the dotted line."

In December of 1983, Carlos Colon again found himself battling for a title, this time for the Universal championship. Colon's opponent was NWA World's Champion, Ric Flair.

For 30 minutes, Flair and Colon were locked in a classic duel. Finally, Colon executed a beautiful Somersault Leap and a Reverse Take Down, and Flair found his shoulders pinned to the mat. Carlos Colon had shocked the wrestling world. He was now the Universal champion.

After winning the Universal belt, Colon began to travel to the States to defend his title. He put his belt on the line in North Carolina, in New Jersey, and even in Texas. Carlos Colon was finally beginning to earn the recognition that he so rightfully deserved.

In February of 1985, however, while defending the Universal title in Massachussetts, former NWA World's champion Dory Funk, Jr., defeated Colon for the title. Colon has nothing but praise for Funk, Jr. "What can I say?" Colon admitted. "Dory Funk, Jr., is an excellent wrestler. He knows every hold in the book and quite a few tricks too. If I was more careful this wouldn't have happened, but I'm confident that I will win the belt back."

At various points in his career, Carlos has been both the Universal Champion and the WWC Heavyweight Champion. He lost the Universal title to Dory Funk, Jr., in February of 1985.

GORGEOUS JIM GARVIN

Weight: 225 pounds
Hometown: Tampa, Florida
Best Move: The Clawhold
Titles Held: World Heavyweight
   Champion

Gorgeous Jimmy Garvin, the flamboyant wrestler from Tampa, Florida, has made a name for himself with both his wrestling ability and his controversial image. Although he isn't one of the largest men in the sport, (he stands just six feet tall and weighs 225 pounds), he makes up for his lack of size by utilizing lightning quick moves and bringing a unique approach to the sport.

When asked to name his best asset, Garvin responded, "my wrestling ability. I can wrestle hold for hold or I can brawl if need be, because I am the greatest wrestler in the world today. I've been wrestling as an amateur since I was nine, and I won my first title when I was 12, so I can wrestle if I feel like it."

Garvin grew up in one of wrestling's famous families, which produced two other wrestlers besides Jimmy. Although no longer active in the sport, Terry is now promoting wrestling in the Central States area, and Ronnie is the current National Heavyweight Champion.

Jimmy started out as one of the most promising wrestlers of his generation when he began his career in Florida. His mastery of Suplexes, Leg Sweeps, and aerial maneuvers made him a crowd pleaser as well as a top-notch competitor who both delighted fans and baffled opponents. Garvin's approach to wrestling involved little hype when he first started out. This purist attitude changed drastically when he took on J.J. Dillon as a manager and advisor a few years ago. Dillon molded Garvin into the wrestler

he is today by refining his wrestling ability and by adding an element of psychological warfare to his act in the form of Garvin's beautiful valet. After wrestling for awhile under Dillon's watchful eye, Garvin was given a valet named Sunshine as a gift for a job well done.

Both Garvin and Sunshine traveled to Texas and took the state by storm as they set out on destroying the Von Erichs one by one. Garvin's battles with the late David Von Erich are legendary, but apparent Garvin victories were overturned by officials who claimed that Sunshine interfered in the match, helping Garvin win and gain the belt.

After Garvin finally won the belt, he gave Sunshine a gift, her own valet named Precious, another striking blonde who assisted Sunshine as she assisted Jimmy. Soon the two women began fighting between themselves, causing Garvin to choose Precious over Sunshine and touching off a bitter feud between the team of Garvin and Precious and the duo of Sunshine and her new boss, Chris Adams.

Their battles raged on and on until Sunshine was injured and forced out of wrestling. Garvin's celebration was premature, as Sunshine's aunt Stella Mae joined the battle in place of her niece

and teamed with Adams to defeat Garvin and Precious in a wild cage match which cost Garvin the title and also drove him out of Texas for good.

Angered by their humiliating loss to Adams and Stella, Garvin and Precious packed up and headed to the AWA, where they immediately challenged World Champion Rick Martel in the ring on national television. Garvin savagely attacked Martel and rammed his head into the steel ringpost after alleging that the champ purposely knocked Precious down in a fit of rage. Garvin's stunt brought about fast results, with Martel openly challenging Garvin to a title match to settle the score for the physical and psychological pain he suffered during the attack.

The many title matches they had were also shrouded in controversy. Garvin pinned Martel several times only to have the decisions reversed because of allegations that he used brass knuckles and other foreign objects to obtain his victories. Garvin feels that these allegations are unfounded, and are simply further evidence that the AWA championship committee is trying to keep him from capturing the world title.

"It doesn't take a wise man to figure out what's going on. It's a

conspiracy. He's being protected by the championship committee. If he wasn't being protected I'd beat him and become the next AWA Heavyweight Champion," Garvin said of the overturned victories.

Besides angering Martel with his antics, Garvin also put Baron Von Raschke in a rage following a televised incident in which Precious was also involved. The Baron had Garvin in his dreaded Clawhold when Precious sprayed air freshener in Von Raschke's eyes, causing him to scream in pain. He fell back onto the mat, where he was easily pinned by Garvin in yet another controversial victory.

Von Raschke has requested a rematch with Garvin because of this incident (which nearly cost him his sight), and has also vowed to pay Precious back for interfering in his match. With men such as Von Raschke, Martel, and others waiting in line to get at Garvin, one would think that Garvin would be worried about the whole thing, but this is not the case. He simply laughs off the many challenges and accusations as jealousy.

"I'm a legendary wrestler," says Garvin. "They're all jealous of me because I'm the greatest looking wrestler alive today. I'm also the greatest wrestler around and I have a beautiful lady by my side when I beat everybody up. I am the greatest wrestler in the AWA and soon I will be the World's Heavyweight Champion. Mark my words." With an attitude like this, Gorgeous Jimmy Garvin will go far in wrestling, quite possibly all the way to the top.

Gorgeous Jim Garvin is a formidable opponent in the ring.

Gorgeous Jimmy Garvin poses with his current valet, Precious. Precious was a gift to Jimmy's original valet, Sunshine, but the two women didn't get along.

Gorgeous Jimmy Garvin once
again proves that he has some
of the best moves in the biz.

HULK HOGAN

Weight: 302 pounds
Hometown: Venice Beach,
 California
Best Move: Media Superstar
Titles Held: WWF Heavyweight
 Champion

Never before in the history of professional wrestling has there ever been anyone quite like the incredible Hulk Hogan.

As soon as the opening refrain of Survivor's hit "Eye of the Tiger" blares over the P.A. system, all eyes are riveted towards the dressing room door. Within seconds, the door swings open and the tall, muscular, 6'8", 302 pound native of Venice Beach, California, makes his grand entry. With his arms swinging wildly, the Hulk approaches the ring. He knows what he has to do to win, and will carry out his mission at all costs. As soon as he steps through the ropes, the Hulk acknowledges the cheers of the faithful by pointing his finger skyward. And the fans go absolutely crazy! In one swift, easy motion, the Hulk rips his Hulk-a-mania T-shirt off his chest and flings it to the crowd, where it is quickly torn into little pieces and savored as a cherished souvenir. The Hulk encounters this phenomenal reaction in every city in which he appears.

But who is Hulk Hogan? How did he become wrestling's hottest attraction? The Hulkster has been wrestling professionally for six years. Prior to entering the ring, Hogan attended college in Florida where he majored in music. Every night, the Hulk could be found plucking the strings of his upright bass in one of the local bars on the Tampa Bay strip. By day, the Hulk could either be found pumping iron or soaking up the

warm Florida rays.

As the Hulk's band began to gain popularity, they soon attracted quite a local following. Two of the group's biggest fans

were Florida's favorite wrestling duo: Jack and Jerry Brisco. Whenever the Briscos were in town, they would invaribly search all over for the Hulk's band. The

brothers were not only impressed by the Hulk's music but also by his immense size and stature.

One day, the Briscos pulled the Hulk aside and asked him if he ever considered becoming a professional wrestler. The Hulk thought they were joking, but after several more similar encounters, the Hulk decided to give it a try. The Briscos then introduced Hogan to former Japanese star Hiro Matsuda. Matsuda taught Hogan the basics of the sport and, once the muscular youngster mastered his teachings, Matsuda booked Hogan in Tennessee.

Soon stories about the sensational youngster began to circulate around the wrestling world. Former wrestling great Fred Blassie was skeptical, but when the glowing reports continued to come in, he flew to Tennessee himself to see what all the fuss was about. And Fred Blassie was very impressed. "The Hollywood Fashion Plate" immediately signed the Hulk to a contract. Blassie put Hulk through a six-month training course during which he taught the muscular giant all the dirty tricks in the book. Once Blassie felt the Hulk was ready, he unleashed his new find on the WWF.

For the next year, the Hulk tore up the WWF and was one of the most despised wrestlers in the sport. It was during his association with Fred Blassie that the Hulk received an offer to go to

Mr. T (left) has wrestled as Hulk Hogan's tag team partner. Hulk (right) has been instrumental in pushing wrestling into the forefront of the American consciousness.

Hulk Hogan shows off his bulging biceps.

A moment of confusion in the ring.

Hulk Hogan gets taken for a ride.

Paul "Mr. Wonderful" Orndorff and Rowdy Roddy meet head on.

"Jeez, don't hit me there"!

Everyone is down, but who is pinning whom?

Rowdy Roddy Piper and Mr. T see eye to eye.

"May I have this dance?"

The ref starts counting Hogan out.

Looks like Rowdy Roddy isn't doing too well.

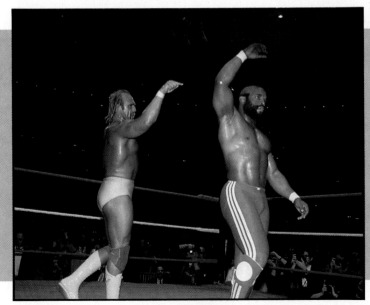

Hulk Hogan and Mr. T parade around the ring in victory.

Who says teammates can't be friends?

Hollywood for a screen test for *Rocky III*. As everyone knows, the Hulk won the part of Thunderlips, and immediately became a Hollywood celebrity. No longer was the Hulk merely "a wrestler." Now he was a bona fide superstar.

During 1982 and 1983 the Hulk wrestled in the AWA. Although he didn't win the title he came very close. As 1983 was drawing to a close, the Hulk re-entered the WWF. This time, the Hulk became an instant hero. The fans rallied around him. The Hulk loved it. After being in the area for one month, the Hulk was matched against the despised Iron Sheik. On January 23, 1984, in front of a sold-out Madison Square Garden crowd, the Hulk annihilated the Sheik to win the coveted WWF Heavyweight title. Hulk-a-mania had arrived!

Since winning the title, the Hulkster has put his title on the line against an endless array of stars. He's clashed with the Masked Superstar, "Dr. D" David Schultz, Paul Orndorff, Big John Studd, The Iron Sheik, Ken Patera, Greg Valentine, Nikolai Volkoff, and most recently, The Magnificent Munaco. Hulk's most celebrated bout was a tag team affair with Mr. T in his corner. These two American heroes took on Rowdy Roddy Piper and Paul Orndorff in the feature bout on WrestleMania. In front of one million viewers, the Hulk and T soundly defeated their arch-rivals in a wild and exciting battle. It doesn't appear that anyone will ever dethrone them anytime soon.

Unlike the image he projects in the ring, the Hulk is very quiet and subdued. He likes his privacy and loves to get away from it all and relax in the Florida sunshine. But with his hectic schedule, such vacations have become virtually impossible.

Hulk Hogan is now the biggest star in the profession and he deserves all the accolades that have been coming his way. He's a fantastic person, a great athlete, and above all, a champion.

Hulk compares his massive, ringed fingers with the smaller, ringed fingers of world famous pianist Liberace (left). Hulk is a friend to many musicians. Grammy-Award winner Cyndi Lauper (right), a big wrestling aficianado, takes some time out of her busy schedule to take a few dance steps with the Hulkster.

KAMALA,
THE UGANDAN GIANT

Weight: 440 pounds
Hometown: Kapala, Uganda
Best Move: Ugandan Belly Flob
Titles Held: None

John Studd, One Man Gang, King Kong Bundy, and, of course, Andre: these are the so-called "giants" of professional wrestling, men with few equals except for one notable exception—the fiercest and most dangerous giant of them all, Kamala, the Ugandan Giant.

Some say that Kamala shouldn't be a wrestler at all, that his upbringing amongst the cannabalistic tribes of his native land presupposes a safety risk each time the big man enters the ring. Perhaps that is true—Kamala is forbidden by law to enter the ring alone; he must be chaperoned in each arena where he appears.

The man who holds the unenviable position of chaperone is Kamala's trainer and long-time companion, his mysterious man Friday. Ever since taking over the reins of Kamala's career, Friday has been forced to conceal his identity (he wears a mask in public) because of the deluge of hate mail and death threats the team receives at their offices from angered fans and opponents. Between fielding the mail and managing his charge's exhaustive training schedule—which often necessitates renting public zoos overnight so Kamala can run wild—Friday more than has his hands full, so Kamala requires additional managerial services.

The responsibility for scheduling Kamala's matches and travel arrangements is a grueling task in itself; only a few top names in management have ever attempted to hold down this

Kamala (right) poses with Animal of the Road Warriors and Skandor Akbar. Few people are brave enough to stand next to the Ugandan Giant.

position, and rarely has one man held on to the job for more than a few months at a time.

"The man's absolutely uncontrollable," says Fred Blassie, who managed Kamala during his first appearance in the World Wrestling Federation in 1984. "I'm no geek, but I gotta admit that he even had me scared once or twice, especially when he's carrying around that spear. One false move, and Jack, you're dead!"

Blassie's not the only manager to have mixed feelings about Kamala, whose spear, ceremonial headgear, and warpaint are enough to send a yellow streak of fear up the strongest spines. Kamala has also been handled at different times by General Skandor Akbar of Devastation, Inc. and British mat star Billy Robinson. Sometimes Kamala's unruly nature has even required the services of both men as well as those of his regular valet, Friday.

"I'm the only man Kamala really trusts," explains Friday. "Over the years we've established a certain bond. Some of his other managers have looked more like a meal to him than a business partner—he doesn't value money. Only his appetite dictates his mood. The man just doesn't listen to reason."

Kamala neither speaks nor understands English, and can communicate only by body language. During televised interviews Kamala is advised to wear a cloak and hood or his tribal mask. He's been known to fly into a rage, attacking every thing he sees: his manager, the interviewer, the camera, the crew, or the entire set.

In the ring, Kamala's awesome presence is even more intimidating. Many opponents are actually too terrified to tangle with

The Ugandan Giant is barely human. Every time he enters the ring, he must be accompanied by a chaperone. He can only communicate through body language. Plus, he's a cannibal.

Kamala, the Ugandan Giant uses the skills he learned capturing wild hippos to subdue a human opponent.

From left to right: Kamala's valet, Friday; Kamala, the Ugandan Giant, and Kamala's former manager, General Skandor Akbar.

Kamala alone, and in handicap matches the giant Ugandan is regularly pitted against two opponents at a time. Even the great patriot Sgt. Slaughter dared not face Kamala alone. He enlisted "Clawmaster" Baron Von Raschke as his cornerman when the time came to meet Kamala in New Jersey's Meadowlands Arena for a "Ugandan Death Match," which the giant won decisively.

When facing top-notch opponents, Kamala's matches almost always get main event status. Andre the Giant, Bruiser Brody, and Slaughter are just a few of the mat stars who have locked horns with Kamala across the country (Kamala rarely limits himself to one wrestling circuit and is one of the most traveled stars in all the mat wars). None were able to convincingly defeat the wild Ugandan. In almost every case a rematch, or more often a series of rematches, had to be scheduled before the burning hot coals of the feud could cool down.

Every time Kamala enters the "squared circle" the ring becomes a jungle. The Ugandan Giant's animal instincts are unleashed, atavistically recalling his youth in the wilds of Africa where he was forced to hunt his own food. As the young Kamala became more adept with a spear, his meals became more frequent and more plentiful. It wasn't long before the Ugandan inflated to the size of the hippoes and rhinoes on which he fed. Instead of growing into a regular man, Kamala grew into a giant.

Kamala quickly outgrew his native land, and began to thirst for adventure. After a stint as a bodyguard for Idi Amin, a role which enabled him to travel with dignitaries and see the world, Kamala decided to pack his bags for the land of opportunity, and he headed for America.

Once in the U.S., however, Kamala found that there were very few jobs for which he was qualified. When he applied for odd jobs, his potential employers would usually tremble at the mere sight of him. Even a career in professional football was out of the question because it was impossible to outfit his gigantic proportions. After a great deal of disappointment, Kamala found what is surely his true calling—professional wrestling.

Despite his lack of scientific training, there is no doubt that Kamala is an imposing figure in the ring. His Throat and Body Chops can devastate an opponent, and once down they're primed for his favorite finishing maneuver, the Ugandan Belly Flop. Like him or loathe him, Kamala is formidable—a force to be reckoned with and a true giant in the world of professional wrestling.

Kamala was once a bodyguard for Idi Amin. When things got tough in Uganda, Kamala packed his bags and headed for the United States.

JUNKYARD DOG

Weight: 260 pounds
Hometown: New Orleans, Louisiana
Best Move: Sheer Brute Force
Titles Held: North American Heavyweight Champion, Mid-South Tag Team Champion

With the sound of "Another One Bites the Dust" blaring over the P.A., Junkyard Dog boogies down the aisle, wildly swinging his chain to the beat of the music. After he climbs through the ropes, J.Y.D. points an accusing finger at his adversary and then gets right down to business. Within minutes, his poor, helpless opponent is lying in a heap on the mat.

J.Y.D. began his rise to fame and fortune in Canada. From there, the Dog traveled to the Mid-South territory, and began to perfect his wrestling technique. "I loved Louisiana," the Dog stated. "The people were great and the competition was superb."

For two years, the Dog was the number one star in the Mid-South. His battles against Hacksaw Duggan, Butch Reed, Nikolai Volkoff, and Kamala were some of the wildest encounters ever seen. "Those guys were some of the roughest in the world," the Dog stated. "But I gave each of them a whipping they won't ever forget."

From the Mid-South, J.Y.D. traveled to the Mid-Atlantic area and soon found himself embroiled in a blazing feud with the wild Oriental, the Great Kabuki. "This Kabuki is one crazy dude," Junkyard stated prior to one of their confrontations in the Richmond Coliseum. "I can't understand how this man can get away with some of the things he

He's down for the count, but has he lost the match? Junkyard Dog is a very determined wrestler, and doesn't like to admit defeat.

does, but he'll get his. I promise you that."

The bout between J.Y.D. and the Great Kabuki was pure mayhem. The Dog had the upper hand throughout the match until Kabuki's manager, Gary Hart, interfered on behalf of his protégé. Once Hart entered the fray, Kabuki completely overpowered J.Y.D., spraying his mysterious green mist in the Dog's eyes. Junkyard passed out cold! Several other wrestlers had to run into the ring to help the Dog.

Following this incident, Junkyard Dog was fit to be tied. In their return bout, J.Y.D. went looking for revenge, and he got it, neutralizing the great Kabuki's mysterious oriental powers by the

sheer brute force.

After the Mid-Atlantic, Junkyard shifted his base of operations to the WWF. And the reception that the Dog has received in the WWF has been phenomenal. Since entering the WWF, the Junkyard Dog has battled all of the big stars in the area and his record has been sensational.

Despite his success the Dog still isn't happy. He wants Greg Valentine's Intercontinental title. So far, the two rivals have clashed on several occasions, but the belt is still Valentine's, thanks to the constant interference of his manager, Jimmy Hart. But J.Y.D. remains undaunted. "Hey, brother, I'm used to his kind. I've run across that miserable Akbar in

Louisiana and that no good Gary Hart in the Mid-Atlantic. But daddy, it doesn't matter to me what he does because the next time he sticks his nose into my business he'll get it good. I've been in this sport too long to let guys like him bother me, and if he messes with the Dog again, he'll be in for some serious trouble."

The stage has been set. The Dog is ready to rumble and he's set his sights on Greg Valentine. Don't be too surprised if, when the smoke clears, another one bites the dust!

Junkyard Dog has set his sights on Greg Valentine's Intercontinental title.

MASKED SUPERSTAR

Weight: 265 pounds
Hometown: Atlanta, Georgia
Best Move: The Cobra Clutch
Titles Held: Mid-Atlantic Tag Team Champion, National Tag Team Champion (with King Kong Bundy), NWA Tag Team Champion (with Paul Jones), National Heavyweight Champion

One of the most devastating wrestlers in the sport is known only as the Masked Superstar. He is a mysterious man who lists his home as Atlanta, Georgia. He stands 6'3", weighs 265 pounds, and cuts an ominous looking figure as he stares across the ring at his opponents through one of his many sparkly masks.

Throughout his career, the Superstar has been both loved and hated by his fans due to his devastating style of wrestling. He can brawl with the best of them, but he can also get down on the mat and wrestle someone hold for hold, executing scientific moves with the grace and speed of someone half his size. Once a match is going in his favor, the Superstar likes to weaken his opponents with Neckbreakers, Flying Tackles, Leg Sweeps, and Clotheslines while setting them up for his favorite finishing hold, the Cobra Clutch. Once he slaps the Cobra on a hapless opponent, his victims slowly fall into dreamland, and victory soon belongs to the Superstar.

His powerful style has brought him fame all over the world. He is especially popular in Japan, where he dominates the competition with his vast array of moves. In the U.S., he has been co-holder of the Mid-Atlantic Tag Team Championship, co-holder of the National Tag Team Championship with King Kong Bundy, co-holder

The Masked Superstar puts his opponent in a Chin Lock.

of the NWA Tag Team Championship with Paul Jones, and also the National Heavyweight Champion. His defenses of the National Championship against men such as Tommy Rich, Mr. Wrestling II, and Paul Orndorff stand as some of the classic confrontations of all time.

After losing the National title, Superstar traveled to the WWF, where he began wrestling for the late Grand Wizard, who touted him as the man to defeat reigning champion Bob Backlund. The Superstar began his championship quest by sidelining Eddie Gilbert after delivering a few Neckbreakers to him during one of their matches. Gilbert's neck was already in poor shape due to an auto accident, but the Superstar's assault severely injured the young wrestler.

This tragic incident foreshadowed the outcome of a title match against Backlund in Madison Square Garden. The Superstar and Backlund battled each other from one end of the ring to the other as they traded

holds and counterholds in an effort to gain an advantage. Soon, the Superstar's strength and size advantage wore Backlund down. But instead of pinning the tired champ, the Superstar chose to toss him out of the ring and give him a Neckbreaker on the cement floor, after which Backlund was counted out by the referee. This move by the Superstar weakened Backlund's neck and was one of the primary causes of his loss to the Iron Sheik in late 1983.

The Superstar hung around the WWF for a few more months challenging Hulk Hogan and giving him some of his toughest title defenses to date. He matched the big man blow for blow and came close to beating him on several occasions. From the WWF he went on to Georgia, Canada, and the Orient before returning to the U.S. to join Sheik Adnan El'Kaissey's stable in the AWA where the Sheik was locked in a bitter struggle with former protégé Jerry Blackwell.

The Superstar wasted no time in joining the fight and giving the

big man everything he could handle. When Blackwell was joined by Sergeant Slaughter, the Sheik countered by pairing Superstar with King Tonga. Tonga and Superstar formed a deadly tag team because of their complementary styles. Superstar uses American-style moves and holds, while Tonga relies on his martial arts training and Oriental nerve holds to gain victories. However, their toughness and rugged nature were not enough to withstand the equally tough team of Blackwell and Slaughter in those brutal, bloody cage matches.

With their battles in the cages behind them, the Superstar and Tonga look ahead to future shots at the Road Warriors and their titles as well as shots against Rick Martel. The duo has a good chance at derailing the Warriors, since they match them both in size and in the brutality department. The Superstar can dish out as much pain as they can take.

The Superstar also has his eyes on Rick Martel, whom he has faced many times in Canada. The Superstar feels that he has the edge over the champion because he is a complete wrestler, able to mix it up instead of just wrestle scientifically. It remains to be seen just what will come of this encounter, but given the Superstar's past championship record and overpowering style, don't be surprised if the Masked Superstar becomes the first masked World Champion.

The Masked Superstar has a wide collection of glittery face masks to wear when he enters the ring. He will only reveal his true identity if he becomes the World Champion.

RICK MARTEL

Weight: 236 pounds
Hometown: Quebec City, Canada
Best Move: All-Around Athlete
Titles Held: Canadian Champion, Australian Commonwealth Champion, Australian Tag Team Champion, Georgia Tag Team Champion, Hawaiian Heavyweight Champion, Pacific Northwest Champion, WWF Tag Team Champion (with Tony Garea), AWA World Heavyweight Champion

AWA World Heavyweight Champion Rick Martel is well on his way to becoming one of the most popular champions in history. The Quebec City native is 6'2", weighs in at 236 pounds of well-sculpted muscle, and takes on all challengers with the same enthusiasm he exhibited when he broke into the sport.

The greatest match Martel ever wrestled took place on May 13, 1983, in front of a sellout crowd at the St. Paul Civic Center when he defeated Jumbo Tsuruta to win the coveted AWA crown. This victory was the culmination of years of hard work and dedication. He and Tsuruta battled each other until Martel surprised the Japanese champion with a Flying Body Press to capture the title.

Martel comes from a family that produced two other wrestlers. Besides Rick, there is Pierre, who is a member of the French Legionnaires, and the late Michele, who died in 1978 after a serious injury suffered during a bout against the Invader and Carlos Colon. Rick's brothers taught him a lot about wrestling and were the driving force behind his decision to turn pro when he was 16. After defeating Tsuruta, Rick dedicated the victory to his

Rick Martel (top) grapples with his opponent, Kendo Nagasaki. Martel is an enthusiastic athlete: He puts his belt on the line against any challenger.

late brother for all of the guidance he had given him.

Martel has held numerous titles throughout the world, including the Canadian Championship, Australian Commonwealth Championship, Australian Tag Team Championship, Georgia Tag Team Championship, Hawaiian

Heavyweight Championship, Pacific Northwest Championship, and the WWF Tag Team Championship. These titles gave Martel the experience and seasoning he needed to wrestle for the world title when he first entered the AWA.

Martel slowly worked his way up through the ranks until he was in line for a match against former champion Nick Bockwinkel. He tried everything he knew to defeat Bockwinkel, but was stopped by the outside interference of Bockwinkel's clever manager, Bobby Heenan. Whenever Martel had the match going his way, Heenan would distract the referee, enabling Bockwinkel to reverse Martel's advantage and score a victory.

Most men would have been shaken by such incidents, but Martel continued to challenge Bockwinkel, hoping to one day defeat him and become champion. This dream almost went up in smoke when Rick was upset by Tsuruta in March 1983 in Tokyo. But instead of abandoning his quest, Martel began training for a match with Tsuruta under the supervision of former champ Verne Gagne, who recognized that Martel had what it takes to be a champion.

The first obstacle in Rick's path was Bockwinkel, who was signed to oppose Martel in an elimination match, with the winner to meet Tsuruta. Martel controlled Bockwinkel for the entire match, and handily defeated him to earn the shot at Tsuruta in May.

After beating Tsuruta, Martel defended his belt against the challenges of Bockwinkel, Saito, and Tsuruta, proving to everyone that he was truly the champion.

His stiffest challenge to date has been Gorgeous Jimmy Garvin and Precious, who have tried every trick in the book to trip him up.

Garvin, an excellent wrestler, relies on psychological warfare to rile Rick. So far, Garvin has accused Martel of attacking Precious and knocking her down, of using brass knuckles to win matches, and of being an inferior wrestler—all charges which Martel denies.

"He's accused me of a lot of things and he's said that I insulted his girl but that's not my style. I would never insult a girl," Martel said. "He also claims that I used a foreign object but again, I don't do that because it's not my style. There's one thing I won't do and that's use cheap tricks to hold onto my belt. I want to be a true champion."

Martel responded to Garvin's charges by challenging him to a title match. Garvin managed to defeat Martel a few times, but the decisions were overturned by the officials, who caught Garvin using brass knuckles to pin the champ. By fighting Garvin many times, Rick discovered his weaknesses, and was soon defeating Garvin on a regular basis.

After defending the title from Garvin's attacks, Martel geared up for future matches against Masked Superstar, King Tonga, and other hungry challengers. Martel has stated that he plans to add ten more pounds of muscle to his body before taking these men on. "If I have to go against Tonga or Superstar I'll have to go against them at 240 or 245 because they're big men. When you wrestle big men the pace is different, and they'll throw you around like you're nothing."

Looking ahead to his future title defenses, Martel wants to be known as a fighting champion who puts his belt on the line against all worthy opponents, not just those he feels he can defeat. "I'm not going to back down from anyone. If I did, I wouldn't feel worthy of the championship. I'll get ready and go out there and mix it up. If I win, that's great. If I lose, I'll just stand up again and fight more to get it back."

Rick Martel shows off his championship belt. Two of Rick's brothers were also wrestlers: Pierre and the late Michele, who died from injuries suffered in the ring.

THE MISSING LINK

Weight: 235 pounds
Hometown: Parts Unknown
Best Move: The Head Thrust
Titles Held: None

Since the dawn of human existence, mankind has attempted to distinguish itself from the animal kingdom by claiming to be of far superior intelligence and ability. But every once and a while a creature is born which can claim to be neither man nor animal, but falls somewhere between the two—a missing link in the evolutionary process. Such a creature has recently made a career for itself in professional wrestling, and this man/beast is appropriately know to mat fans as The Missing Link.

If The Missing Link could talk, oh, the tales he could tell. Even simple information like his place of birth and family background could prove priceless to pioneering biologists. If only more was known about the Link, new chapters could be written in the science books—but The Missing Link cares nothing for science, a fact he makes clear each and every time he enters a wrestling ring.

The Missing Link has entrusted his future entirely to the ring strategist known as the "Bossman," Percival Pringle the III. "I don't know what it is everyone's so concerned with—the man's a professional wrestler," says Pringle of his mysterious protégé. "And a damn

The Missing Link is truly one of a kind. With his green makeup, random tufts of hair, and primitive mind, the Link is a terrifying sight in and out of the ring. He eats live alligators, too.

good one at that. Any other theories are mere speculation. The Link's no beast, he's a tender, loving soul."

Maybe to Pringle he is tender and loving, but this description tells us nothing of the Link's biological makeup. It seems that Pringle is intentionally dodging inquiries, since The Missing Link could easily be banned from wrestling at a moment's notice.

The other popular theory about The Missing Link is that he was once a successful and renowned wrestler who flipped his lid after suffering severe injuries in the ring. This possibility is supported by the Link's superbly conditioned musculature. However, the fact he uses no established wrestling holds would lead one to believe that he's forgotten everything he may have once known about the art of grappling. In any case, even a casual observer of The Missing Link's ring style would have to conclude that there's more than just a small element of insanity in his behavior, and he's undoubtedly lost at least part of whatever mind he ever had along the way.

One thing The Missing Link hasn't lost is his excellent physical conditioning. The reason for his strength, according to Pringle, is the Link's commitment to the "Back to Nature" fringe in professional wrestling. The Link trains for his match exclusively in the out-of-doors, and feeds on a well-balanced diet of raw flesh, fruits and vegetables. Because of his eating habits, Florida is the ideal location for the Link's wrestling career, since the exotic mat star is particularly fond of the taste of chewy alligator hide. With this in mind, Pringle has astutely arranged for the Link's feeding

time to correspond with his training sessions, as he encourages his charge to hunt and kill his own gators before devouring them.

"Catching his own meals keeps him in shape, and it keeps him in touch with his roots, too," says Pringle. "The man's gonna be a champion one day, since I wouldn't handle anything but, and he's got to be tough inside the ring and out."

It's pointless to question Pringle's managerial ambitions, since he's already proven himself a maker of champions. Since arriving in the Sunshine State in early 1985, the "Bossman" has been the guiding light behind Florida State Champion Jesse Barr and Southern Champion Rick Rude, as well as the tag team combination known as the Pretty Young Thing Express, which has battled for the Southern Tag Team Title with Mark and Jay Youngblood. Pringle's ultimate goal is to round up every Championship Belt in the state of Florida, and he doesn't have far to go. The next step would be to send a contender up against Ric Flair for the World's Heavyweight Title, and The Missing Link may be the man he's got in mind.

There's no question that The Missing Link is a qualified competitor, since he's just about wiped up the ring with every opponent Florida promoters have put him up against. Lately they've been coming slower and less willingly, afraid to face the mysterious Missing Link in the ring. His mere appearance, with green facial paint and odd tufts of hair, make him ready for war, and only a fool would believe that it's a war he has even the most minute chance of losing.

But for those who do have the courage to enter the ring with The Missing Link, the best strategy is to use their heads before the Link gets a chance to use his. Since The Missing Link is severely lacking in scientific mat skills, he uses what comes to him naturally, namely his rock-hard forehead, and Pringle has labeled this one-weapon arsenal the Head Thrust. Pringle has found that the best way to condition his charge for these deadly butts is by giving his man a steel chair which he can slam into his skull for hours on end until the steel thins and the bottom falls out.

In the ring, the Head Thrust has a more profound effect on The Missing Link's opponent than it does on steel chairs. Poised on the second ring rope or turnbuckle, an opponent becomes no more than a target at which the Link aims his devastating Head Thrust. Whether it is aimed at another head, a back, a chest, or a stomach, the Head Thrust has the ability to knock its victim out cold. It's believed that The Missing Link may have the hardest head in all of wrestling (a physical throwback to the Stone Age) but Percy Pringle refuses to comment on this subject, once again fearing that his charge might be banned from the mat wars.

Due to Pringle's secretive policy, it's doubtful that any more information on The Missing Link will ever come to light, but it's really of little consequence. Whether he's just a mentally ill maniac or the scientific specimen his name implies, the only thing one really needs to know is that The Missing Link is a dangerous and explosive creature terrorizing the Florida wrestling circuit.

DUSTY RHODES

Weight: 301 pounds
Hometown: Austin, Texas
Best Move: The Bionic Elbow
Titles Held: NWA World
    Champion, WWF Champion

Dusty Rhodes is less a wrestler than a phenomenon. To say this is not to denigrate his ability but to express what his career has been all about. Every match he wrestles is a personal crusade in defense of the American Dream.

To understand how Rhodes came to be cast in the role of avenger, it's necessary to return to the start of his wrestling career. He was one of the most feared rulebreakers in wrestling, infamous as one half of the dreaded Outlaws, a brutal tag team (Dirty Dick Murdoch was the other half). The Outlaws wrestled like crazed monsters. If an opponent could walk out of the ring without help, the Outlaws felt they'd failed. Nobody wanted to wrestle the Outlaws; why not walk in front of an 18-wheeler on the interstate instead?

Not surprisingly, tragedy occurred. Dusty beat a young preliminary wrestler mercilessly and snapped his spine in two. This wrestler's identity remains one of the sport's best kept secrets; Dusty has sent so many men home on stretchers that investigators can't figure out exactly who this man was. In the interests of his family's privacy, the victim remains anonymous.

The incident changed Dusty Rhodes' life. Like many other misguided patriots, Dusty had assumed that it was necessary to use force in the pursuit of honor and success. Rhodes was making it, climbing the ratings, and earning a bundle of money. He

was proud of himself. But when he paralyzed a young man who had a family, his pride turned to shame.

The transition from rulebreaker to fan favorite did not adversely affect his career. He still wrestled with the power and tenancity of a bulldozer. Stan Hansen, no slouch of a ring commando himself, called Dusty his toughest opponent because of his durability, recalling, "Once I hit him over the head with a chair, and he just kept comin' at me with the chair dangling around his neck!"

Rhodes engaged in one of the bloodiest feuds in wrestling history when he tangled with Superstar Billy Graham in a lengthy series of grudge matches in the NWA and WWF; Graham,

too, was trying to attain an American dream, but his dream and Dusty's dream clashed with the sickening thud of foreheads. By the time their feud finally petered out, as a result of Graham losing his WWF title and subsequently pursuing a passive Eastern philosophy, both men were lucky to be alive.

Dusty Rhodes has been one of the foremost competitors in wrestling for the past ten years. Rivals have snickered at his jive rap and obese physique. But he can teach hard lessons in the ring, and his fanatical determination has been the key to his success. He's fighting for the fans, he's fighting for America, and he's fighting for the kid he paralyzed.

But is he fighting for himself?

Critics have taken careful note of the astonishing amount of punishment Dusty's taken. It's a safe bet that no wrestler has spilled more blood in battle than Dusty Rhodes. It's even been suggested, by his detractors, that he bleeds if you look at him hard. And some of Dusty's closest friends and admirers wonder if he sees himself as some kind of martyr atoning for the sin of the wrestling world, specifically the horrors caused by rulebreaking. He is, some fear, still attempting to atone for the sins he himself committed as a rulebreaker.

Whatever his motivation, Rhodes has won the NWA World's Title twice. He lost his first title only because he demanded to wrestle with a broken leg. He pinned Ric Flair for the unofficial "Lord of the Ring" title, an honor no wrestler has shared since. Currently, he holds the NWA TV title, one of the most significant belts in the sport.

Dusty Rhodes has achieved the dream of his early days. Rumor has it that he may retire soon to devote his full energies to promotion and TV work. However, one thing is certain: No one in wrestling has put more of himself into the sport than Dusty Rhodes. At this point, and after all he's been through, he'd probably view digging red clay under a broiling sun as a vacation.

Dusty Rhodes (left top) in the ring: a dynamo. Early on in his career, Rhodes crippled a young wrestler. Ever since, he has atoned for his sins by wrestling on the side of law and order.

SERGEANT SLAUGHTER

Weight: 302 pounds
Hometown: Parris Island, South Carolina
Best Move: The Cobra Clutch
Titles Held: Mid-Atlantic Champion, U.S. Champion

"I pledge allegiance to the flag of the United States of America. . . ." By reciting this simply oath into the ring announcer's microphone, one of professional wrestling's most feared and despised ring warriors was able to cash in his bad reputation for a loyal fan following.

The timing just happened to be right for the millions of Americans who were looking for someone or something to believe in. Someone they could look to for leadership, who would not desert them in the heat of the battle. Someone who would stand up for truth, justice, and the American Way every time he entered the ring. And the man to fit the bill was the "All American Hero," Sgt. Slaughter.

At the outset of his wrestling career, Sgt. Slaughter was a bitter man, discharged from the Marine Corps for excessive cruelty to his troops in boot camp. As the Sarge turned to wrestling for his livelihood during the Vietnam era, many Americans took an immediate dislike to the abrasive Sergeant: He represented everything that was wrong with their country.

As one of the WWF's most detested villains, Sgt. Slaughter repeatedly waged war with champions Bruno Sammartino and Bob Backlund, always falling just inches short of the Heavyweight Championship. Slaughter further enraged WWF fans by insulting Andre the Giant and facing off against the popular

With his Army fatigues and flags, Sergeant Slaughter is one of the most aggressively patriotic wrestlers in the sport.

Frenchman in mortal combat. For all this and more, the fans gave Sgt. Slaughter the nickname "Gomer" and ridiculed him in one arena after another.

Knowing where he wasn't wanted, the Sarge packed his duffel bag and headed for the Mid-Atlantic area with high hopes of winning a championship. Before long he had set his sights on the U.S. Title, a prestigious belt which he has now held on two occasions.

In October of 1981, the Sarge won the strap in an elimination tournament in Charlotte, N.C. But, alas, there was virtually no one in the crowd willing to cheer him on.

"I suppose they were still scared of me then," says Slaughter now. "At the time I was concentrating on hurting people first and foremost; I hadn't yet established my patriotic bond with the American people."

The man Slaughter had the most difficulty with was Indian Chief Wahoo McDaniel, who was well-loved throughout the Mid-Atlantic area. In May of 1982 McDaniel caught Slaughter off guard and claimed the U.S. Belt for himself—until a leg injury prevented him from defending the title against Slaughter in June. The Sarge was awarded the belt by default, thus beginning his second title reign.

Sgt. Slaughter defended his cherished U.S. Championship with valor for most of the summer of '82, but the Mid-

Early in his career, Sergeant Slaughter simply concentrated on hurting people. It wasn't until 1982 that he established his patriotic bond with the American people.

Atlantic fans still refused to warm to him. By August the tide had turned again, when Wahoo McDaniel returned to reclaim the U.S. Title. A beaten man, the Sarge turned to a fellow American for support, and he and (Pvt.) Don Kernodle became a devastating tag team combination that captured the NWA World's Title in September of '82 at a tournament in Japan.

Time certainly flies in the world of wrestling, and two years can sometimes seem like decades. Now the Sarge is quite possibly the most popular man in the sport today, and Kernodle, since abandoning former tag team partners Ivan and Nikita Koloff, is known as the "Pride of the U.S.A." Such was not the case in late '82 and early '83, however, when the aggressive U.S. veterans terrorized the entire National Wrestling Alliance. Finally, in March of '83, Slaughter and Kernodle were defeated by Ricky Steamboat and Jay Youngblood in a brutal and bloody steel cage match in Greensboro, N.C.

By this time brutality had become old hat to the Sarge, and when he returned to the WWF later that year he vowed to use any means within his power to capture the Heavyweight Crown. But once again the crowds chanted "Gomer," and the Sarge grew hot around the collar and

was distracted from his mission. Then a series of events took place which forced Slaughter to reassess his role in the world of professional wrestling.

Early in '84 Sgt. Slaughter announced that he was organizing a demolition crew, which he named the Cobra Corps after his famous finishing maneuver, the dreaded Cobra Clutch, and he inducted the young Terry Daniels as its first member. But in the meantime another clutch was taking hold of the WWF, the notorious Camel Clutch of Ayatollah Blassie's main man, the Iron Sheik.

Ever since the hostage crisis, the Sarge had harbored a deep hatred for the Iranian people, and a natural tension developed between the two grapplers. Finally, when the Iron Sheik took a cheap shot at Daniels, the Sarge had no choice but to declare war.

"That Iron Sheik and Blassie went a little too far when they started picking on my boy," recalls Slaughter. "I felt it was my patriotic duty to put those maggots in their place."

What followed was possibly the most violent series of battles WWF fans have ever witnessed, culminating in a climatic "Boot Camp Match" at Madison Square Garden in which both men were beaten to pulp before Slaughter finally covered the hated Sheik for the pin.

Kamala, The Ugandan Giant (left) is the victim of Sergeant Slaughter's ruthless attack.

This dramatic feud and its photo finish had sealed Slaughter's new reputation as wrestling's all-American war horse, and the readers of *Pro Wrestling Illustrated* voted the Sarge "Inspirational Wrestler of the Year" for 1984. Slaughter's reputation and his standing with the fans had made a 360-degree turnaround. But while he was loved wherever he went, always handing out flags and signing autographs, the Sarge still couldn't get himself a title shot against WWF Champion Hulk Hogan. Frustrated, he left the WWF in early 1985 to seek his fortune in the new combined NWA/AWA affiliation known as Pro Wrestling U.S.A.

Since joining Pro Wrestling U.S.A. the Sarge has gotten his wish, and has challenged Ric Flair on two separate occasions for the NWA World's Heavyweight Championship. Both times Flair suffered a beating, and the Sarge won decisive moral victories—but unfortunately Slaughter was disqualified each time for minor infractions of the rules. There's a good chance that Slaughter and

Flair will be meeting again in the future, and the Sarge is hoping that this time he'll be leaving the battlefield with ten pounds of gold wrapped around his waist.

In the meantime, Sgt. Slaughter has been doing his patriotic duty for pro wrestling, making sure that the squared circle is safe once again for American wrestlers, and his primary feuds have been with Kamala the Ugandan Giant and Sheik Adnan Al Kaissey's rulebreaking crew.

"As long as there's scum in the world endangering the American way of life, you can bet that the Sarge will be there leading the fight," pledges Slaughter. "And I won't stop short of a complete victory."

You'd hardly know the Sarge was talking about wrestling....

Sergeant Slaughter (right) throws his opponent into the ropes. The Sarge is no stranger to brutality.

Sgt. Slaughter puts a Neckbreaker on the Iron Sheik. He takes special delight in trouncing the Sheik and his Russian teammate, Nikolai Volkoff. Iran and the U.S.S.R. are not countries the Sarge admires.

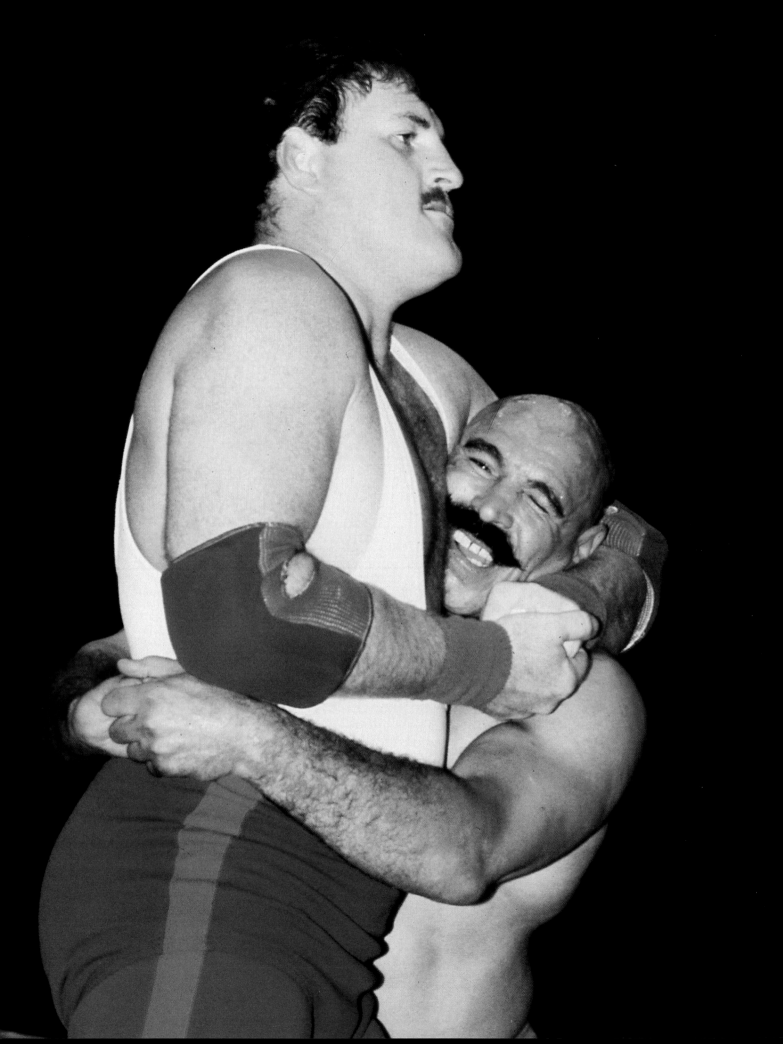

KEN PATERA

Weight: 275 pounds
Hometown: Portland, Oregon
Best Move: The Swinging
    Neckbreaker
Titles Held: AWA Tag Team
    Champion, Mid-Atlantic
    Champion, WWF
    Intercontinental Champion,
    Missouri Champion, Georgia
    Heavyweight Champion

There are many men who claim to be the strongest wrestler alive, but few can back up their claims like former Olympic weightlifter Ken Patera. The Portland, Oregon, native is 6′3″ tall and weighs in at 275 pounds of solid muscle. He has traveled all over the globe, taking on all challengers in an effort to prove his supremacy in wrestling.

Patera started out his career as a powerlifter and shot putter, winning gold medals in the 1968 Pan American Games in Mexico City. He followed up these victories by winning a bronze medal in weightlifting at the 1972 Olympic Games in Germany, beating out top lifters from East Germany and the Soviet Union. Patera is very proud of his accomplishments as a weightlifter and enjoys talking about them whenever he has a chance. He is also the first man ever to military press 500 pounds.

After the Olympics, Patera had his pick of sports to compete in, and chose wrestling over football and baseball because of his love for one-on-one competition. He entered Verne Gagne's wrestling school in Minnesota and became one of the school's most famous grads, entering the AWA rings right after completing the grueling program. He started out as an ultra-scientific wrestler who stuck to the rule book and used his strength to his advantage in a lawful manner.

When Patera noticed that he was going nowhere by being clean, he resorted to using dirty tactics to win matches, and he hurt people when he felt like it. These tactics were panned by the press but they enabled Patera's career to skyrocket faster than he ever imagined. He was hated wherever he appeared but that didn't bother him. His championships included the AWA Tag Team Championship, the Mid-Atlantic Championship, the WWF Intercontinental Championship, the Missouri Championship, and the Georgia Heavyweight Championship.

When Patera entered the AWA in 1982, he joined the Bobby Heenan Family, where he tag teamed for awhile with Bobby Duncum, Nick Bockwinkel, and John Studd as they tried in vain to beat Greg Gagne and Jim Brunzell for the titles. Heenan and Patera got along well, since they shared a hatred for the Gagnes— Verne and Greg. They joined forces to rid wrestling of the popular father and son duo every chance they got.

Patera's accomplishments impressed Sheik Adnan El'Kaissey, who paid $500,000 for his services as Jerry Blackwell's tag team partner. The Sheik paid Heenan $250,000 for Patera's contract, and gave another $250,000 to Patera for signing on with the Sheik and teaming with Blackwell. This team took the AWA by storm. They not only won the belts but also crippled anyone who tried to stop them.

After losing the titles in mid-1984, Patera dropped out of sight due to an injured knee suffered at the hands of Crusher in the title loss. After he had healed sufficiently, Patera surfaced in the WWF under the guidance of Captain Lou Albano, who groomed him for title matches against Hulk Hogan. These matches never took place, because Patera suddenly signed on with Heenan, who had moved to the WWF suddenly after being suspended from the AWA for life. Patera was soon joined by Studd, who wanted to join his old friends in their plot to destroy Andre the Giant.

Their secret plan was revealed in a televised tag match when they took on Andre and S.D. Jones. Andre and Jones controlled the match for awhile until Jones was thrown out of the ring when he missed a punch meant for Patera. With Jones lying unconscious outside the ring, Patera and Studd went to work double-teaming Andre, and beat him until he was also unconscious. Heenan then jumped into the ring with a pair of scissors and directed his men to cut off Andre's hair.

All three men took turns clipping away. When their dirty deed was done, they stuffed the clippings in a plastic bag and left the ring smiling and holding Andre's hair aloft for all to see. Their assault on Andre not only humiliated the giant but also left him with a concussion that kept him out of wrestling for a while. During Andre's absence, Patera, Studd, and Heenan proclaimed an end to Andre and celebrated their apparent victory.

Their celebration was cut short when Andre quickly returned to action and set his sights on Patera in hopes of paying him back for the pain he had suffered as a result of his unscheduled haircut. Their match, scheduled for Madison Square Garden, was billed as Andre's revenge, and that's exactly what it was. The giant dominated Patera with a ferocity never exhibited by him before. Heenan stood by watching as the giant smiled while beating Patera into oblivion. When the going got too rough, Patera slipped out of the ring only to be followed by Andre, who continued his assault outside the ring to the delight of the sellout crowd.

Patera managed to get in a few shots at the angry Giant but they were to no avail. The Giant was out of control, torturing Patera as he had never tortured anyone before. Patera and Heenan finally managed to escape to the dressing room, thereby forfeiting the match to Andre but managing to stay in one piece. After the match, Patera and Heenan still claimed superiority over Andre by accusing him of using rulebreaking tactics in the match.

Patera has since dropped his vendetta against the Giant and is now training hard for a shot at Hulk Hogan and the WWF championship. In his career, Patera has challenged Bruno Sammartino and Bob Backlund for the WWF title, Harley Race and Dusty Rhodes for the NWA title, and Verne Gagne for the AWA title without ever winning the championship. Maybe now is the time for Ken Patera to put all his abilities together and take a shot at Hulk Hogan.

The highlight of Ken Patera's career took place during his match with Andre the Giant. Patera and Big John Studd beat Andre unconcious, and then, with the help of Bobby Heenan, cut his hair.

JIMMY "SUPERFLY" SNUKA

Weight: 260 pounds
Hometown: The Fiji Islands
Best Move: The Superfly Leap
Titles Held: U.S. Heavyweight Champion, Pacific Northwest Heavyweight Champion, NWA World Tag Team Champion

Simply amazing! That's the only way to sum up the most incredible move in professional wrestling—The Superfly Leap, as perfected by Jimmy "Superfly" Snuka.

For sheer grace and agility, they don't come any better than Snuka. "The man is simply unbelievable!" stated his one-time manager, Captain Lou Albano. "If he had only listened to me, Jimmy Snuka would be champion to this day, but that's another story. Today, Superfly Snuka is finally getting his act back together. He's on the right track, and don't be surprised if someday you even see us in the same corner."

It's an outrageous prediction, but it just might come true. Like the Superfly, Captain Lou Albano has also reformed, and the two now even share the same dressing room. But don't think for a second that their past differences have been forgotten. There was too much bloodshed between Superfly Snuka and Captain Lou Albano for them ever to forget the past.

For those unfamiliar with the Superfly saga, a little background information is needed. Captain Lou Albano was the man instrumental in bringing the Superfly to the WWF. Although Snuka rarely if ever obeyed the

Jimmy "Superfly" Snuka can fly—the first man since Superman to boast such a skill.

rules, his incredible physique, smooth moves, and amazing Superfly Leaps endeared him to the fans. It wasn't long before Snuka was getting more cheers than boos.

The turning point in Snuka's career occured on the TV show Buddy Rogers' *Corner*. During the interview segment, Rogers told Snuka that Captain Lou Albano had stolen all of Snuka's money. Albano immediately denied the claim but couldn't produce the bank books, C.D.'s, and stocks that he had supposedly put in Snuka's name. The two soon came to blows, with Albano enlisting the aid of Ray Stevens and Fred Blassie to launch an unprovoked attack in front of millions of TV viewers.

From that moment on, the Superfly was loved by one and all. For the next year, Superfly Snuka continued to fly to great heights, chalking up victory after victory with his amazing moves. But suddenly and without warning, the Superfly came crashing down to earth. The culprit this time was Roddy Piper. On a segment of *Piper's Pit*, Snuka suffered total humiliation when Piper smashed a coconut over his head, knocking him totally unconscious. Piper then proceeded to smear a banana in Snuka's face. This incident was to be the start of a war that has yet to be resolved. Following this humiliation, Snuka suffered further injury in a match when Piper smashed a chair over his head. Snuka suffered several cracked vertebrae in his neck and was out of action for months.

Right now, the Superfly is ready to take off. Although he was grounded temporarily by "Rowdy" Roddy Piper, Snuka is now prepared to sail to great heights once again. With the Superfly's amazing talent, it's only a matter of time before Roddy Piper finally gets what he deserves.

Jimmy Snuka, a superstar of wrestling, meets Muhammad Ali, a superstar of boxing.

ROWDY RODDY PIPER

Weight: 235 pounds
Hoometown: Glasgow, Scotland
Best Attribute: Superior Intellect
Titles Held: Mid-Atlantic Champion

Trying to describe Rowdy Roddy Piper in a few paragraphs is like trying to explain World War II in a thousand words. Or turning Shakespeare's collected works into a TV mini-series. Or splitting atoms with a nail file. Roddy Piper is much bigger than life; he's bigger than wrestling. And he's only just begun his career.

You could hardly have forecast Piper's tremendous impact on the sport if you had witnessed his first professional match. He was a skinny, precocious braggart whom promoters tried to teach a lesson by matching against Larry Hennig. Hennig weighed more than two Roddys, and pinned him in ten seconds. Promoters didn't realize that Roddy Piper is, for better or worse, indomitable; major setbacks are minor irritations to him, easily brushed away and forgotten like dandruff from a jacket. Roddy fully intended to command wrestling, to shape it like wet clay in the jittery hands of a mad sculptor.

After a brief apprenticeship in the prelim ranks, Piper first caught the wrestling world's attention in Southern California (which, in the late '70s, enjoyed a much livelier scene than it does at present). Piper blasted through the area like plague in a rat colony. The fans had never seen anything quite like him. The guy was barely past the legal drinking age, and not only was he winning titles right and left but he was *managing* the most successful rulebreakers in the region! As successful as he was in guiding the careers of Bad Leroy Brown,

Crusher Verdue, and the like, critics charged he was neglecting his own career. It foreshadowed a recurrent problem for Piper. In trying to dominate all facets of the sport, he risked short-circuiting his championship potential.

And make no mistake about it, it wasn't just Piper's personality that woke up the sport. You'd need a roomful of hands to count the number of amateur titles he had won, and he knew how to mix amateur stylings with the most effective professional maneuvers—Suplexes, Neckbreakers, Piledrivers, etc. Piper's wrestling genius shone through in the Mid-Atlantic league, where he captured the coveted U.S. Title from none other than Ric Flair. It was the greatest match of his career, and a short route to a world championship was anticipated.

In the fall of 1981, Piper began to divide his attention between grappling in the Mid-Atlantic and doing color commentary on *Georgia Championship Wrestling*. Piper proceeded to astonish viewers with his insights. He lambasted fan favorites and praised himself incessantly, but it was his broadcasting style that really disgusted viewers—the barbaric, shrill, stream-of-consciousness banter that WWF followers are now familiar with. Despite all the criticism, Piper is responsible for liberating wrestling's television journalism establishment.

Piper was on the verge of being lynched from a peach tree when he suddenly cast himself in the role of savior. The program's host, the venerable Gordon Solie, was pursuing a probing line of inquiry with the Magnificent Muraco, whom Piper had hired as a bounty hunter to eliminate Tommy Rich. Muraco, then at the apex of his distinguished career, took a few pokes at Solie (who has suffered from hip and leg trouble for quite a while), and Piper rushed in to defend the

Rowdy Roddy Piper is one of the most intelligent and mercurial wrestlers working today. His TV interview program has set new standards in wrestling broadcast journalism.

Captain Lou Albano, Cyndi Lauper, and Rowdy Roddy Piper: His Piper's Pit *has changed the face of wrestling broadcasting.*

broadcaster. Not long before that, Piper had been stabbed by an irate fan in a parking lot, and Roddy surfed on a wave of sympathy in the Mid-Atlantic. All of a sudden, he began to praise fan favorites on the tube and fired Muraco. What was going on here?

Piper has, throughout his career, ricocheted back and forth between two steel walls—fan favorite and rulebreaker. Whichever attitude he chooses, it must be an extreme—he never straddles the fence of fan acceptance. Having studied crowd behavior as a psychology major at a Canadian university, he loves to manipulate the fans. When he was stabbed in the parking lot, he worked it to his advantage by leaking to the press that he had been trying to save a bunch of schoolkids from a knife-wielding maniac! In the light of recent developments, the story has been

discredited. Piper's inconsistency has cost him countless fans—no one trusts him.

Of course, Piper became a national celebrity on the basis of the rock/wrestling controversy. This superfeud, which is very far from being over, has simultaneously rejuvenated and depressed wrestling. Unfortunately, Piper shares most of the blame for the fiasco. It was a lousy idea to invite a thoroughly unqualified guest like Cindi Lauper on *Piper's Pit*. And for the first time, confidants of the Rowdy Scot began to fear for his sanity. Their concern was activated by Piper's wrestling "style," which currently bounces back and forth between total lethargy and near-epileptic seizures of violence. Piper is one of the natural strategists in wrestling, and he knows how to make a strategy work. Perhaps driven half-blind in the glare of publicity (which is

more like a hate campaign against him), Piper is punching, kicking, and gouging rather than maiming with his customary skill and grace.

Greg Valentine won his belt by beating Piper's left ear into submission with it, spurring one of the ugliest feuds in recent history. Piper lost 75 percent of the hearing in his ear, and fans were aghast that the blood-soaked belt could change hands on a foreign-object submission. Their war culminated in a spectacular "Dog-Collar-And-Chain Match" that nearly ended with two corpses in the ring.

Soon afterwards, Roddy Piper entered the WWF. Roddy's dominance of the federation was all-encompassing, and his brilliance and wit turned heads upside down. His versatility was incredible. He managed a stable which received title shots almost immediately after they entered the

WWF. He still wrestled, and most importantly, he hosted the most provocative wrestling feature on television, *Piper's Pit*. The Pit was like a punch in the stomach. It combined philosophical insight and caustic humor.

One thing is certain: Roddy Piper can be a World's Champion if he wants to be. He's battered Ric Flair once before, and he can do it again; Hulk Hogan would be no match for him if he evolved the proper game plan for cutting down the big man. If he can sidestep potential assassins, he's got a long career ahead of him. And he'll be assaulting legends and other secondhand porcelain sacred cows along the way. Love him or not, Roddy Piper is a revolutionary force in wrestling.

While in the ring, Rowdy Roddy Piper vacillates between periods of sheer, manic craziness and dull, lifeless lethargy.

RICK STEAMBOAT

Weight: 225 pounds
Hometown: Honolulu, Hawaii
Best Move: The Drop Kick
Titles Held: World Tag Team Champion, U.S. Heavyweight Champion, Mid-Atlantic Heavyweight Champion

Dynamic, exciting, and sensational are just a few of the choice adjectives that have been used to describe "the Happy Hawaiian," Ricky Steamboat. The Honolulu native is simply the best all-around wrestler in the sport today. There isn't a hold that Steamboat hasn't mastered nor a move that he can't execute. His timing is perfect, his leaps are astonishing, and his Drop Kicks—superb. Combine this with his well-rounded scientific knowledge and you have a complete professional.

"I learned the basics of the sport several years ago in one of Verne Gagne's training camps," Steamboat remarked. "I always wanted to be a professional wrestler and after I learned that Verne Gagne ran a wrestling camp for aspiring professionals, I wrote and inquired about joining. I stayed there for several months and finally graduated into the pro ranks."

After wrestling in the AWA for a few months, Steamboat traveled to the Mid-Atlantic league. It was there that he literally put it all together. "My first few months were torture," Steamboat admitted. "I knew what I had to do in the ring to win but things just weren't working out right. Hey, everyone wants to be an overnight success. I did, too, but it didn't happen that way. It takes years to make it in this profession."

During the first few years in the Mid-Atlantic, Ricky won and lost the Mid-Atlantic TV title and the World Tag Team belts. Eventually, he locked horns with the U.S. Heavyweight champ, Ric Flair. It was the start of a rivalry that has spanned the entire length of both their careers. Over the years, these two have faced each other innumerable times. Early in

At one point, Rick Steamboat was the U.S. Heavyweight Champion.

their careers, the U.S. belt and the Mid-Atlantic Heavyweight belt bounced back and forth between Steamboat and Flair.

But after Flair captured the NWA World's title, Ricky Steamboat's luck seemed to run out. "It's frustrating," Steamboat admitted. "I would love to win the World belt but sometimes it takes more than talent to win the crown and I won't take anything away from Ric Flair. He's a great champion. He's worked hard to get to the top and he deserves the belt. But deep down inside I feel I can beat him."

In January 1984, Ricky Steamboat was at the crossroads of his career. For seven years, the

Hawaiian had toiled in rings all over the world, gaining an international reputation and a following second to none. But Steamboat was tired—the constant traveling was wearing him down. It was then that the popular Steamboat decided to pack it all in. "I had just opened a gym in Charlotte and I just couldn't be away for weeks on

The Happy Hawaiian puts his moves on Ric Flair.

end. After much thought I felt it was best to devote my full time and energies to the gym."

Steamboat's fans were brokenhearted. How could their hero desert them? For the next five months, Ricky Steamboat stayed away from the spotlight but eventually the wrestling bug bit again. It took some persuasion from Jay and Mark Youngblood and even Ric Flair to get Ricky back into the ring, but the moment he agreed to put the tights back on, his friends knew he would be back for good.

After Steamboat's comeback, he was scheduled to meet his number one rival, Ric Flair. Their match in Greensboro, N.C. was

one of the greatest battles of all time. The two fought toe to toe, and if it wasn't for the 60-minute time limit, the two rivals would still be battling today. After his comeback match against Flair, Steamboat was to battle the NWA World's champion to eight more one-hour draws. "Ricky Steamboat has to be my toughest opponent," Ric Flair has stated on many occasions. "The man is simply phenomenal. There isn't a move that he hasn't mastered."

Several months after his return bout against Ric Flair, the Hawaiian defeated tough Dick Slater for the U.S. Heavyweight belt. Steamboat held on to the U.S. belt for several months before losing it to another old rival, Wahoo McDaniel.

After wrestling in the NWA for seven long years, Ricky Steamboat joined the WWF in January of 1985. Since entering the WWF, Ricky Steamboat has moved himself right to the top. His remarkable skills and sensational moves are now turning on a whole new legion of followers. The South Pacific Connection, a tag team featuring Steamboat and Jimmy "Superfly" Snuka, is well on the way to becoming one of the most popular tag teams in WWF history.

Wrestlers like Ricky Steamboat only come along once in a great while. With his remarkable talent, the Happy Hawaiian, Ricky Steamboat, will continue to amaze fans for many years to come.

Rick Steamboat and Ric Flair traded the U.S. belt and the Mid-Atlantic Belt back and forth many times early in their careers.

HARLEY RACE

Weight: 260 pounds
Hometown: Kansas City, Missouri
Best Move: The Hanging Suplex
Titles Held: NWA World Champion

It was Indian summer, and Harley Race scraped his twice-broken nose against the beige pillowcase. He stood there in front of a picture window overlooking the Mississippi riverfront, as the first orange rays of the sun struck East St. Louis, Illinois.

Harley Race took off his shirt. "Go ahead, punch me in the stomach," he calmly stated. "Punch that flab as hard as you can. You'll find out why I'm champion. I can't be punished. You can't hurt me." The kid aimed for Race's hairy belly. He wanted to make the World's Champion gasp and beg for mercy. He ran towards Harley Race, hitting him with such force that he fell down. Race helped the kid up off the floor and sent him on his dazed way.

For an inexperienced wrestler, going up against Harley Race is like engaging the gods in mortal combat. Nights get long for the kid who faces Handsome Harley in the morning.

Harley Race can't be beaten. Sure, every once in a while he gets pinned. But he never gets whupped like a dog. He never whimpers back to the barracks with his tail tucked. You can't clobber him, and it's conceivable that you can't even *hurt* him without resorting to a foreign object.

Harley Race lost his very first wrestling match. The lucky man was named Bill Koll, a proud individual who can tell his grandchildren, "I pinned Harley Race in his first match."

The bruises accumulated as Race tallied up the matches. One night in St. Paul, he crossed

Harley Race is one of the most refined, skillful wrestlers in the sport.

mugs with Larry Hennig and one of the most devastating tag teams in history emerged. Handsome Harley Race and Pretty Boy Larry Hennig held the AWA World's Tag Team belts for four years and broke enough bones to pave a sidewalk.

Race's defensive wizardry stems from an incident in a 1969 chain match. Terry Funk deprived Race of 15 percent of the vision of his left eye with a length of rusty chain. Wrestlers cannot survive in the ring without top-notch peripheral vision. As a result, Race has had to develop an especially keen intuition, an almost parasensory sense of impending danger. Harley can detect a move three seconds before you've thought about it, and that, more than anything else, is the key to his success.

The feud with Terry and Dory Funk, Jr., lasted for nearly a

decade, until Race won the NWA title from Dory in 1973. He lost it quickly to Jack Brisco, and then changed his style in favor of a more aggressive attack. For some reason, Race's first, brief title reign was discredited by the media. The prevailing outlook was that Harley's championship was a fluke, sheer happenstance. The popular press failed to appreciate the subtleties of Race's wrestling skill. Like any modern artist, he was accused of fraudulence. Race was attempting mat perfection before an indifferent audience.

Race had to act fast. He stopped bleaching his hair and started splintering bone and marrow in his quest for the golden championship belt. The first bone to splinter was Terry Funk's. He never fully recovered from his leg fracture at the mercy of Race's Indian Deathlock—he still hobbles when he thinks

nobody's looking. Although Harley nearly crippled one of the sport's greatest talents, he got his second title reign, and you better believe it was worth it!!!

Harley Race epitomized wrestling from 1977 to 1981, until a brash iconoclast named Ric Flair took command of the title. Race won and lost the belt five times in that period, but the beltless gaps in the calendar were little more than vacations. Dusty Rhodes, Shohei Baba, and Tommy Rich shrank back from Race's skill and cunning. Harley made everything look as easy as unlacing a shoe.

After Race lost to Rhodes for the second time, he started to hear the skeptics again. "Harley, you're through," they'd hiss, and smart men who should have known better professed to wonder why Race had won six NWA World's titles. Race proved the so-called experts wrong on June 10, 1983, when he defeated Ric Flair for his seventh title reign.

Harley Race has never been a wild animal in the ring. He has never put his image ahead of his work; he's there to wrestle, not pose. Watching him in the ring, you can tell the fans are a continent away in Race's mind; he neither taunts them nor encourages their cheers. In fact, he doesn't acknowledge them at all. His mission is ring perfection, and he very nearly attains it. No one has mastered more holds and strategies than Race. The man doesn't have a nickname (which is almost unheard of in this sport), but he commands the finest gimmick of them all: greatness.

A brutal bout with Terry Funk in 1969 left Race with 85 percent vision in his left eye.

JIMMY VALIANT

Weight: 240 pounds
Hometown: New York City, New York
Best Move: The Hanging Suplex
Titles Held: WWF Tag Team Champion (with Lucious Johnny Valiant)

Jimmy Valiant proceeds to destroy the hapless Great Kabuki.

No matter the city, state, or arena, the appearance of this man never fails to bring the house noise to a crescendo. The man from New York City stands for ring justice, and puts forth his best effort when the match is a brawl. "It's my specialty," says "Boogie Woogie Man" Jimmy Valiant, "and it works."

Born and raised in the Big Apple, Valiant participated in amateur wrestling all through his school years, but many of his ring techniques were learned in the city streets. Jimmy began his professional career as "The Body" in Texas, then assumed the title of "Handsome" Jimmy when he moved onto the home scene of New York and WWF territory.

Jimmy didn't have the patience to settle for a slow road to stardom, so he switched roles: from Texas fan favorite to New York rulebreaker. He hoped the new image would hasten his climb to fame, and for the same reason he signed sports great the Grand Wizard as his manager. The Wizard's leadership techniques were often a cause for speculation, but he set out to create champions and he usually succeeded.

He did not, however, succeed with Jimmy, who, when his contract expired, ventured to Japan and then to AWA territory. All the same, before long he was back in New York to unite with his two brothers, also members of the profession.

One brother, Lucious Johnny, was at that time competing under the guidance of one Captain Lou Albano. Jimmy also signed with Albano, and he and John were a formidable partnership, capturing the WWF Tag Championship in 1974. Shortly thereafter they were joined by the third Valiant, Gentleman Jerry. Jimmy then co-managed his brothers with Albano. The team was successful, but future contract negotiations with Albano were not, and the association broke up. John and Jerry set off for Japan; Jimmy opted for Memphis.

In Memphis, Jimmy found himself back in favor with the fans, and in violent opposition to the rulebreakers. With or without a championship belt, he was destined to become the people's champion. It was here that he was dubbed the "Boogie Woogie Man."

Valiant began traveling between the NWA territories of Memphis and the Mid-Atlantic, and he seemed to meet controversy at every turn. Sir Oliver and his House of Humperdink were Boogie Woogie Man's priorities in the Mid-Atlantic. Needless to say, Sir Oliver didn't take kindly to Jimmy's plans to destroy his kingdom, and he contracted Ivan Koloff to halt Valiant's crusade. Night after night and match after match, Jim went heads on with the Russian Bear. The battles were long and bloody, but Jimmy was still standing when Ivan's agreement with Humperdink came to an end. Jos De Luc was then assigned to Valiant, and a $100,000 bounty offered to any man who could rid wrestling of Boogie Woogie Man. But wrestling still has Jimmy Valiant; and Sir Oliver still has his hundred grand.

Jimmy can also attest to how a few words spoken in anger, even without malicious intent, can erupt into war. He admits that his comments about the Great Kabuki constituted a low blow—he said he'd like to take off Kabuki's makeup and show the world just how ugly he was. Kabuki's facial disfigurement is a source of deep-seated emotional and mental pain, and nothing could have prompted a more violent reaction from the man who spews the potentially dangerous green mist. The resulting exchange between the two men will be long remembered. As Jimmy once said of words spoken in anger or otherwise: "You can't take it back, so you face up to it."

Jimmy's most notorious encounters have probably been with Paul Jones and his stable. Jones has only recently been able to remove the cast on his arm which resulted from his getting too close to Jimmy's "old lady"— not his wife, but the trusted hickory ax handle he uses for "attitude adjustments." Paul sports numerous large, ugly scars from surgery to repair damage inflicted by Valiant.

In an attempt to get back at Valiant, Jones instructed his men to lose no opportunity to attack Valiant. During a bout, Jones' men Superstar Billy Graham and the Barbarian were inflicting brutal punishment on their two young opponents. Their intent was injury, not pin fall. Jim, true to his quest, went to their rescue. He entered the ring and smacked his "old lady" across Superstar's back. Barbarian joined the fracas, but when Jim went to swing the Barbarian glanced the blow with his forearm and knocked the ax handle from Jim's grasp. As they punched it out, Jones crawled into the ring on the opposite side and retrieved the stick. Swinging with everything he had, Jones planted it firmly in Jim's rib and kidney region. As the Barbarian locked Jim's arms, Jones and the Superstar each took an end of the handle and with as much force as possible rammed the stick into Valiant's throat.

The dressing rooms seemed to empty into the ring as Jones and his men made a hasty retreat. Valiant was carried from the ring and rushed to the hospital.

Jimmy Valiant is now fully recovered and Jones will live to regret his actions. However, Jones is a dangerous commodity and has sworn to put an army in any city where the Boogie Woogie Man appears. He certainly won't have to chase Mr. Valiant. Such threats are unlikely to put Valiant on the run; he's not one to run away from a fight.

"The Boogie Woogie Man" Jimmy Valiant started out as a fan favorite in Texas. Impatient for stardom, he moved to New York, where he became a rulebreaker. Now he's popular with the fans again.

BIG JOHN STUDD

Weight: 364 pounds
Hometown: Los Angeles, California
Best Move: Reverse Bear Hug
Titles Held: Mid-Atlantic Tag Team Champion (with the Masked Superstar)

One of the most imposing figures in wrestling today belongs to the 6'9", 364-pound giant from Los Angeles named Big John Studd. Studd has made a career out of claiming that he is the only true giant in wrestling, and has twice challenged Andre the Giant for the title of wrestling's true giant.

Studd's greatest asset is his height, which makes it almost impossible for any normal-sized person to scoop him up and slam him to the mat. While an opponent is busy trying to lift him into the air, Studd plants a few fists to their back, rendering them helpless as he softens them up for his dreaded Reverse Bear Hug. Once Studd picks up an opponent and wraps his mammoth arms around his victim's torso, the poor man cries out in pain, and Studd adds another victory to his long list.

John Studd has a long list of impressive credentials, which include the Mid-Atlantic Tag Team Championship with his partner the Masked Superstar. While in the AWA, Studd and Crusher Blackwell injured The Crusher's shoulder and knocked him out of wrestling for more than a year. The list goes on and on, but the one incident Studd is especially proud of is the time when he, Ken Patera, and Bobby Heenan gave Andre the Giant a concussion and an unsolicited haircut.

When Studd entered the WWF for the first time, he was managed by Freddie Blassie, who guided the giant toward title shots at both Bob Backlund and Andre the Giant. Blassie even went so far as to hold weekly contests on television to see if any wrestler or fan could body slam Studd in the center of the ring. (Studd claimed that no one could slam him

At 6'9", Big John Studd is one of the tallest grapplers around. His height makes it almost impossible for anyone to Body Slam him.

because of his height.) The prize for accomplishing this feat of strength was a cool $10,000. The money stayed with Blassie since no one was able to slam Studd or even lift him off of his feet.

The only person who came close to slamming Studd was Andre when he unexpectedly took Jay Strongbow's place as the scheduled "slammer of the day." Both Studd and Blassie were visibly upset at seeing Andre walk down the runway and into the ring. When Andre was set to pick up Studd, Blassie grabbed onto Studd's waist and tried to hold him down. Andre tried to lift him twice and as he hoisted him up the second time he noticed Blassie holding on for dear life. Angered, Andre charged Blassie, grabbed the $10,000 from him, and began tossing it to the spectators. Studd sneak-attacked Andre and took the money from him and ran into the dressing room with Blassie.

This incident touched off a bitter feud between the two giants. They battled all over the WWF and finally settled their differences in a cage where Andre put an end to Studd's bragging by not only beating him but by slamming him in the center of the ring. This humiliation drove Studd out of the WWF for a short time until he returned in 1984 to rekindle his feud with Andre.

This time he aligned himself with good friend Ken Patera and former AWA advisor Bobby Heenan. Together, the three thought up a devious plan to humiliate Andre by destroying him so that he would quit wrestling and retire. Their plan came to a head when they triple-teamed him during a tag match with Andre and S.D. Jones. After they had beaten Andre unconscious, Studd, Patera, and Heenan cut off Andre's hair in the center of the ring. This display of barbering was reminiscent of Samson being sheared in Biblical times, when the Romans cut his hair to sap his strength.

After celebrating their apparent victory, they were surprised when Andre returned to wrestling after a short absence to seek his revenge on Studd and his friends. The two giants had many memorable, blood-filled matches. Their feud came to a head during the much celebrated WrestleMania when Studd and Andre faced off in a special $15,000 "Body Slam Match." The rules were simple:

Paul "Mr. Wonderful" Orndorff (left) and Big John Studd show off their impressive physiques.

Andre would win the match and $15,000 if he could body slam Studd in the center of the ring. If he was unable to slam Studd, Andre would retire on the spot and never return to wrestling.

Excitement ran high as Studd walked to the ring accompanied by Heenan, who carried a small gym bag loaded with $15,000. Andre was met with a chorus of cheers as he entered the ring and smiled wryly at Studd and Heenan. The action was nonstop as Andre took the initiative by working on Studd's legs with a series of kicks and knee drops. He soon shifted his attack to other areas of Studd's body including his arms, back, and torso, as he softened him up for the match-ending slam. When he felt that he had tortured Studd enough, Andre hoisted up the big man and drove him to the canvas with a loud thud, Andre then claimed his cash reward and threw some out to the fans before Heenan jumped into the ring, snatching the bag from Andre and running away with most of his $15,000.

To this day, Studd maintains that he was not cleanly slammed and that Andre cheated when he slammed him. Studd is currently training for more title matches against Hulk Hogan. He has met Hogan and defeated him by count-out, leaving Hogan bleeding and semi-conscious outside the ring. Studd's follow-up encounters were just as bloody and wild, and he again came close to pinning the champ and winning the gold belt.

The battles between Studd and Hogan were classics because they fought for not only the title but also for prestige of being the strongest big man in wrestling. In their last match they fought down to the wire, but Hogan managed to hang onto his belt by slamming Studd outside the ring on the concrete floor, causing him to lose by a countout. This decision may have ended the Studd/Hogan feud for now, but with Heenan directing Studd's every move, we may once again see Big John Studd challenge either Andre or Hogan for WWF supremacy.

Big John Studd is currently out to get Hulk Hogan. Studd looks pretty threatening—Hogan had better be on his guard!

From right to left clockwise: Manager Buddy Heenan, Ken Patera, and Big John Studd—a truly terrifying trio that numbers among the most dangerous men active in the sport today.

KERRY VON ERICH

Weight: 260 pounds
Hometown: Denton, Texas
Best Move: The Von Erich Claw
Titles Held: Texas Tag Team
Champion (with Bruiser Brody),
World Heavyweight Champion

To say that the future of wrestling lies in its young is hardly original, but one look at this man and you will understand the truth of the statement. His spectacular physique, raw talent, ambition, drive, and fortitude would seem to make him equal to any task set before him. He has been beaten—but never defeated. He is a Von Erich, and they seem to be made of particularly strong stuff—they always bounce back.

In school Von Erich concentrated on track and field, with his main efforts being directed toward the discus throw. In high school he won the State Championship and, when attending the University of Houston, went on to break the national record. Naturally enough, he had his sights set on the Olympics, but had to change his plans when the United States declined to attend the 1980 games. So it happened that Kerry followed his father, Fritz, and brothers David and Kevin into the ring.

His interest in weight lifting was both inspired and guided by pointers from such notables as Ken Mantell and Arnold Schwarzenegger, and he responded to their encouragement. He wasn't just a young hopeful; he had real determination. He puts in at least an hour a day at the gym six days a week in order to strengthen his already proven ability.

Kerry's first appearance in the ring offered clean evidence that he had no place to go but up. In no time his partnership with Bruiser Brody saw him in the winners circle as half of the Texas Tag Champions. Then on January 1, 1983, he took the Missouri State Championship from Harley Race. This one was going to be his ticket to Ric Flair.

After his Missouri victory, some people predicted that Kerry's anxious anticipation of the World's Title would be his downfall. They figured that if he neglected the job in hand in anticipation of future glories, he would lose not only the title he already held, but also the opportunity to capitalize on it. As it turned out, his critics underestimated him.

In 1982, Kerry did indeed face Mr. Flair, with the "ten pounds of gold" at stake. He didn't win that night, but he did not give up the quest. He was to meet Flair on three later occasions—only to be beaten each time by some infraction of the rules.

The last of these three contests was a cage match with Freebird Michael Hayes as the referee. Hayes, trying to aid Kerry, decked Ric from the rear and invited Kerry to go for the pin. Kerry refused to accept the victory and Hayes, displeased, turned to leave. Trying to get Hayes' attention, Kerry made the mistake of turning his back on Flair, who took advantage of the moment and planted a knee to Kerry's back, sending him cannoning into Hayes with enough force to knock Hayes from the cage door. Terry Gordy saw the fall but not its cause, and assumed Kerry was attacking Hayes. He lifted the cage, smacking it into Kerry's head. Kerry lost so much blood that the match was stopped.

Kerry's attention was temporarily diverted from Flair to the Freebirds, and his brothers David and Kevin were ready to take their places as contenders for the World's Title. There is, however, no competition within the Von Erich family. They share the battles and the victories. Kerry did not relinquish his championship ambitions—he only passed them on to his brothers for a while. David, though, never got his chance to face the champion. He died suddenly in February 1984 while on tour in Japan. Kerry's deep sense of loss over his brother's death deepened his determination to win the next time he faced Flair.

The opportunity came in Texas Stadium on May 6, 1984. Kerry Von Erich won the World's Heavyweight Championship. Afterwards he said, "I did it for David. It may sound strange but I could feel him in there with me. This is in memory of him."

For the next 18 days Kerry squared up against some of the toughest contenders in the sport, and he stayed on top. Then he went to Japan. Flair made the trip, too, to challenge Kerry for the title he felt he should never have lost. Ric Flair reclaimed his belt by beating Kerry in two out of three falls on May 21. Kerry offered no excuses, but David's failure to return from his trip to Japan only a few months earlier had to be weighing heavily on his mind.

Even when Flair isn't around, Texas is never dull. Kerry recently vowed to silence Gary Hart's rantings about how his "One Man Gang" was immune to the Von Erich Claw. The behemoth Gang had steel plates in his head as a result of street fights, Hart boasted, and the Claw could not hurt him. Kerry took up the challenge. He planted his hand on Gang's forehead and stepped up the pressure. With an ordinary man the effect would have been evident immediately, and it was only a matter of minutes before the Gang was trying to pry Kerry off. Hart, sensing defeat, flew into the ring and poked Kerry in the eyes, breaking the hold. Bedlam ensued, but the Gang knew he'd been in trouble. Hart has still not found the answer to the Claw.

A significant factor in Kerry's life has been the Von Erich split with Chris Adams, once a close family friend. At present the conflict is at its most violent between Kevin and Chris, but Kerry is always close in case Chris should resort to foul play.

The Von Erichs are to wrestling what oil wells are to Texas. Kerry has earned the respect of his peers. He promises to be a major wrestling force for years to come.

As a member of a world-famous wrestling clan, handsome Kerry Von Erich has had to work hard to escape the shadow of his family name. Now, having won the World Heavyweight Championship, Kerry has earned the respect of both his fans and his fellow competititors.

KEVIN
SULLIVAN

Weight: 230 pounds
Hometown: Boston, Massachusetts
Best Move: Hypnotism
Titles Held: Southern Tag Team Champion (with Mike Graham)

Gadzooks! What is that man doing with those snakes in the ring? Is this a wrestling match or a circus sideshow? And why is he dragging that scantily clad woman around on a leash? And why is she wearing real bones around her neck? What's this all about, anyway?

What *is* it all about? That's what the fans want to know. But the only answer they get from the wrestler is that he follows the "Powers of the Darkside." To put it another way: He's an avowed Satanist.

The man—though there's some question about whether he's mortal—is Kevin Sullivan. He's the single most frightening force in professional wrestling today. Dozens of wrestlers use gimmicks to give themselves a psychological edge in the ring, but Sullivan's routine is the most dangerous because it's the most real. At least, Sullivan believes it's real, and that's usually enough to scare away most of the cynics.

Sullivan insists that both his physical strength and his psychic powers come to him directly from the Oracles of Abughdadian, the sixth of the 66 legions of Bael, the ruler of the underworld. Most people would talk about the forces of evil linked to the mythical Satan, but it offends Sullivan to have his beliefs trivialized.

"Bael does not like to be called by his common name," says Sullivan of his spiritual leader. "Do you call a king 'Bub?' No, Bael is the supreme lord of lords, and from him all knowledge flows. Bael in turn enables Abughdadian to impart wisdom to

me in the form of the betel nut. Chewing on its leaf, the powers of the darkside are revealed. With these powers as a point of reference, the world of wrestling is mine for the taking!"

Ominous words, and they're amplified by Sullivan's strange presence. The self-proclaimed "Prince of Darkness" rarely appears in public without his mystic war paint—usually black lines, crosses, and pyramids drawn on his forehead—and as well as a large "X" shaved in his chest hair to represent an inverted crucifix carved in his heart. This bizarre sight is enough to scare off most opponents.

It hasn't always been that way. Sullivan began wrestling when he was only ten years old, and wrestled in amateur competitions for eight years, all through his studies at Boston University where he studied management. During his amateur career the young grappler took six YMCA titles in the Boston area, and twice won the Boston Schools Championship.

The year after he graduated from B.U., Sullivan worked some small wrestling circuits and earned several regional titles in both singles and tag team competition. By the end of 1971 Sullivan was ready to make a bid for national notoriety, and he set up camp in Florida. When he arrived in the Sunshine State he teamed up with Mike Graham, and the two soon took the Southern Tag Team Championship. The popular pair held the title for over a year, then lost it in a bout in which Eddie Graham was forced to substitute for his injured son: The Samoans gave Sullivan a thrashing he would long remember. Even then Sullivan, who was still relying on scientific skills, must have realized that dirty tactics often

prevail in the mat wars.

In an effort to improve his appearance rather than his approach, Sullivan began to devote most of his time and attention to working out in the gym.

"Kevin approached his workouts with almost religious fervor," says Mike Graham of his former tag team partner. "This was a time when most wrestlers didn't bother with body building, and Kevin's weight training was way ahead of the game. In just a few years he had developed one of the most impressive physiques in all of professional wrestling."

But after reaching the pinnacle of health and fitness, Sullivan suddenly started to let himself go. His hair and beard went untrimmed for months and grew increasingly unruly. His once well-toned stomach began to protrude and jiggle as he moved. His reaction time in the ring became slow and lethargic. His fans watched in amazement as one of their favorites, most muscular mat stars deteriorated before their eyes. What had happened to the promising young athlete? No one could understand the transformation.

It was then that Sullivan made the announcement which hit the wrestling world like a ton of bricks: He was dedicating his life to the worship of Satan!

"All the know-nothings in the material world thought that I had gone soft, but in reality I had made the only intelligent choice. My initiation into Abughdadian was a harrowing time for me, and I was forced to sacrifice long hours in the gym for an intensive philosophical realignment. But what is worth more, a body which will one day rot in the earth's soil, or spiritual wisdom which lasts a thousand lifetimes?"

Since his conversion to

Satanism, Kevin Sullivan has exercised a hypnotic effect over other wrestlers both in and out of the ring, and over the past few years he has assembled a cult which at times has included Jake "The Snake" Roberts, Maniac Mark Lewin (whom Sullivan attired in a monk's robe and affectionately nicknamed "The Purple Haze"), Hacksaw Jim Duggan, Buzz Sawyer, Superstar Graham, and other, more mysterious characters like Kharma, Molokai, and the Reverend Black. Once under Sullivan's spell, each of them became a zombie-like in devotion to their prince, obeying his every whim and willing to follow their master to the grave.

Sullivan also enjoys the company of women, and numbers several in his entourage. If Sullivan's involvement with dark powers remains an enigma, his relationship with his women is equally strange. His two most visible companions, Fallen Angel (formally known as Angel Dust), and the seductive Lock, are two temptresses who seldom appear clad in much more than a skimpy bikini. And Sullivan certainly doesn't view his women as equals, preferring to dominate them as a man his dogs. He often escorts his "pets" into the ring on a leash, and relishes having them grovel at his feet.

Is Sullivan really possessed by some demon, or is he actually a psycho? It's hard to draw any conclusions about his career except on his own terms, and by his own account the devil made him do it.

Believe it or not, this terrifying-looking man was once a straight-arrow wrestler. Now, he's an avowed Satanist.

GREG VALENTINE

Weight: 243 pounds
Hometown: Seattle, Washington
Best Move: The Figure-Four Leglock
Titles Held: U.S. Champion, ICC Champion

More than any other sport, wrestling has witnessed a number of father/son combinations. Fritz Von Erich and his offspring, Bob and Brad Armstrong, Warren and Nick Bockwinkel, Bruno and David Sammartino, Blackjack Mulligan and Barry Windham...as TV personality Joe Franklin would say, "The list is ENDLESS!" One of the greatest father/son combinations of all, however, is that of Handsome Johnny Valentine and his son Greg, *AKA* "The Hammer."

Although he never won a World Title, Johnny Valentine was one of the sport's all-time greats, and a barbaric master of the Atomic Skullcrusher. A virulently hated rulebreaker for most of his career, Johnny was a thinker as well as a crippler. He once invited a bloody feud with ex-NFL stars Ernie Ladd and Wahoo McDaniel because he accused them of intellectual deficiency. "Football is for idiots," he said. "Wrestling is the sport of the intelligentsia."

Like any athletic progeny, Greg Valentine was haunted by his father's greatness. He didn't help matters any by dubbing himself "Johnny Valentine, Jr." early on in his career. Greg had to bully his way into respectability to scoot past his father's shadow. Another problem that intensified Greg's fighting spirit was the unusually small size of his hands and feet. Scouts and promoters doubted his ability to grasp a bigger opponent, and some other wrestlers taunted the youngster about it. To compensate, Valentine worked hard on developing a potent Elbow Smash that would utilize the beefy power in his thick biceps and upper arms. (He has since refined his style, and now uses the elbow sparingly, preferring to concentrate on more complex maneuvers.)

It didn't take long for Valentine to bash his way into contention. Although he has wrestled around the globe many times over, he has enjoyed by far the greatest success of his chosen profession in the WWF and Mid-Atlantic regions. Mid-Atlantic fans, in particular, have grown to hate Greg with a passion for his cruel dominance of the area. He has won the U.S. Championship Belt (the second most important title in the NWA, next to the World's Title) many times; it's like a special toy he picks up and discards at will.

The yellow brick road on the way to his title reigns has been littered with bloody bandages and hospital X-rays. His legendary wars with Wahoo McDaniel have sent both men to the emergency room countless times; after breaking Wahoo's leg with the Figure-Four Leglock, Valentine strutted to and from the ring with an "I BROKE WAHOO'S LEG" T-shirt. (Johnny Valentine, whose own career was prematurely shortened by injuries sustained in a plane crash, undoubtedly encouraged his son's vendetta against Wahoo.)

The most notorious atrocity Valentine committed in the Mid-Atlantic was winning the U.S. Title by deafening Roddy Piper with his own championship belt. The sad spectacle of Piper staggering around semiconscious with blood pouring out of his ear and down his neck made Valentine snicker with delight. Later that year Greg was designated "Most Hated Wrestler" in the 1983 *Pro Wrestling Illustrated* Readers' Poll, the third time he had captured that distinction. Only Ken Patera, a double conferee, has won it more than once. When it comes to alienating the fans, Valentine has few peers.

Valentine has been one of the pre-eminent forces in the WWF since he first appeared there in 1979. Aided by the supernatural wisdom of his manager The Grand Wizard, Valentine won the coveted Intercontinental Title and came *very* close to beating then World Champion Bob Backlund on numerous occasions. In fact, Valentine was awarded the World Title after one controversial match with Backlund, but the decision was reversed on a technicality. Greg knew how to endear himself to folks in the Northeast—his creed has always been maim, and maim again.

"I love to hear the sound of a kneecap or shinbone crunching when I cinch down the Figure-Four Leglock," Valentine once said, and he proved it again in the WWF. This time his victim was saintly Chief Jay Strongbow, whose patented Kneelift just hasn't been the same since the night they had to carry him off in makeshift splints. Insiders say that Valentine is prouder of breaking Strongbow's leg than of winning the U.S. and ICC Titles.

Presently, Valentine is in the midst of his second WWF Intercontinental reign. After long and tedious months of trying to break previous champion Tito Santana's leg, Valentine settled for taking away his title and sending him in for arthroscopic knee surgery.

At his best, Valentine is an extraordinary wrestler. He knows how to put the hurt on. Far from relying upon rulebreaking to win matches, he also uses his considerable scientific repertoire. Valentine has one of the best Double-Underhook Suplexes in the business, and the Figure-Four is not his only way to torture limbs. In fact, he specializes in attacking the limbs, and can hurt you just as badly with a dazzling variety of Armlocks and Indian Deathlocks. Unless his anger has been aroused, Valentine is a methodical craftsman of pain in the ring.

However, Greg Valentine needs a manager to harness his talent and provide strategic guidance. Although he's adept at devising intricate and torturous means of hurting limbs, he often fails to put this speciality into practice. He's great when he's in charge, but his defensive skills are below par. He also has the tendency to take risks in a match when he's ahead. Valentine needs the steadying influence of men like The Grand Wizard and Captain Lou Albano to perform at his peak. It remains to be seen whether recently acquired manager Jimmy Hart will serve him as well as in the future.

If Valentine smartens up and concentrates totally upon the style that suits him best, watch out. He is gifted with greatness, and his finest years are most likely ahead of him.

Greg Valentine's prowess is genetic. He's the son of all-time great wrestler Johnny Valentine.

THE FABULOUS ONES: STAN LANE AND STEVE KEIRN

Weight: 465 pounds (combined)
Hometown: Del Ray Beach,
   Florida
Best Move: Speed and Agility
Titles Held: Mid-Southern Tag
   Team Champions

Two of the biggest crowd pleasers in tag team wrestling are Stan Lane and Steve Keirn, more commonly known as the Fabulous Ones. Hailing from Del Ray Beach, Florida, they fit the typical image of Floridians—blond, well-built, and deeply tanned. Although they are a small team (weighing in at a combined weight of 465 pounds), they make up for their lack of size with years of experience, fast moves, and complementary styles of wrestling.

Their good looks and flashy images give them the appearance of male strippers rather than professional wrestlers, and they are often mobbed by throngs of young women who are attracted to their handsome looks and well developed bodies. Their youthful good looks and sex appeal anger many of their opponents, who nevertheless find it difficult to defeat the men they call "pretty boys."

Lane and Keirn were not always the close friends they are today. As a matter of fact, years ago they were mortal enemies and battled each other in many blood-filled matches. Jackie Fargo brought them together six years ago, and they've been a smashing success ever since.

After touring the South for a few years and dominating the tag team scene there, they packed their bags and headed north to the AWA where they set their sights on the Sheiks: Ken Patera, and Crusher Blackwell. At that

Steve Keirn punches Hawk right in the gut.

time, the Sheiks were running roughshod over everyone, and the Fabs believed that their speed and agility were enough to topple the powerful Sheiks. They spent hours and hours working out in the gym preparing for their series of matches with the Sheiks only to be crushed when the champs were upset by the team of Blackwell and Baron Von Raschke.

The Fabs had to settle for wrestling in a series of preliminary bouts while waiting for a shot at the new champs. While waiting their turn, they became embroiled in a bitter feud with Nick Bockwinkel, Mr. Saito, and their manager Bobby "The Brain" Heenan. This deadly threesome thrashed the Fabs, injuring Keirn's neck when he was pile driven on the cement floor. Bockwinkel, speaking for his team, said that he didn't like the Fabs' style and wanted to rid the sport of the "male stripper" element they brought to wrestling.

Lane continued to battle Heenan and his men alone while Keirn recuperated. On Keirn's return, they quickly eliminated their rivals and taught the trio that even though the Fabs look like

His blond hair flying, Keirn delivers the finishing touches.

go-go dancers, they wrestle like pros. Although both men are experienced grapplers, Bockwinkel and Saito were no match for the more experienced Fabs, who baffled them with quick moves and slick teamwork.

Following their efforts against Heenan's boys, the Fabs were given a title shot at the Road Warriors, who had just defeated Crusher and Von Raschke in a controversial match in Las Vegas. The awesome size of the Warriors contrasted with the Fabs' speed and agility, and the match proved to be a memorable one. Both sides traded the advantage back and forth until the Warriors eventually took control, thanks to both their size advantage and a little outside help from their ever present manager, Precious Paul Ellering.

Angered at Ellering's constant interference, the Fabs took matters into their own hands and asked the Crusher to be their advisor. The Crusher coached them in the necessary brawling techniques. After adding some meanness and a few dirty tricks to their repertiore, the Fabs were more successful against the

Warriors, but were once again thwarted by Ellering's interference.

Frustrated by their inability to win the belts, the Fabs and Crusher backed the Warriors and Ellering into a corner and finally managed to beat them. The Fabulous Ones left the AWA in early 1985 but not until they took one last shot at the Warriors in a wild action-packed match in Chicago. The Fabs entered the ring wielding metal chairs with which they pounded the Road Warriors' heads.

They battled the champs for close to 20 minutes before Hawk finally put their title hopes to rest when he pinned Lane after a brutal Clothesline. Tired, hurt, and angry, the Fabulous Ones quietly left the AWA and headed back to Tennessee where they hoped to regain their stature as one of the top teams in the South. Their return was met with loud cheers from their many fans who had waited for the day when their heroes would return home.

Even though the Fabs failed to win any World Tag Team titles, they should not be thought of as losers. They battled the Warriors with everything they had but unfortunately they still were defeated. Together for six years, the Fabs have set a record for tag team longevity, and they are still considered one of the top teams in the sport. If the Fabulous Ones continue to work and to win, they just might achieve their dream: the title.

The Fabulous Ones, Steve Keirn and Stan Lane. Labeled "pretty boys" by their critics, this agile, powerful team can inflict a lot of damage in the ring.

THE FREEBIRDS:
BUDDY ROBERTS, TERRY GORDY, AND MICHAEL HAYES

paired off—it seemed as if the match would soon be over.

But then Killer Kahn interfered with a near-lethal chop. Hayes flipped Kerry and pinned him. The Freebirds were awarded the belts. But upon reviewing the video tape, the World Class officials once again upheld the Von Erichs' title. A six-man steel cage match was signed; surely this would settle things.

Once again, the match took place in Texas Stadium. The wrestlers entered the cage and began immediately. Gone were any pretensions of "pure" wrestling—it was going to be a blood-soaked brawl to the finish, with both teams kicking,

Weight: 730 pounds (combined)
Hometown: Atlanta, Georgia
Best Move: Recording the hit record, "Bad Street, U.S.A."
Titles Held: National Tag Team Champions, Georgia Tag Team Champions, World Class Six-Man Tag Team Champions

Michael Hayes may be the only man ever to wrestle Ric Flair for his NWA World's Title *and* have a hit single in the same career. In fact, for a while it looked as if Hayes would leave wrestling for a career in rock 'n' roll.

It all makes sense. Hayes is the charismatic frontman of The Fabulous Freebirds, a tag team that would easily make minced meat out of any New Wave sissies. They've already destroyed countless grapplers in Texas, Georgia, and Florida. "There's no reason," Hayes bellows, "that my golden locks and beautious bod shouldn't caress the cover of a hit record, daddy. There's no reason why I couldn't strut my stuff right to the top of the hit parade! I'm from Bad Street, U.S.A. ya know, where the boys know how to rock! I am a rock 'n' roll party!"

Was Mr. Peacock Strut going out on his own? The fans listened carefully—some with delight at the prospect of no more Freebirds, some with grave concern. No one was indifferent. Everyone knew that if Hayes went off to rock, it would be the end of wrestling's most flamboyant threesome.

Long before any ideas of rock stardom infiltrated Hayes' bleached-blond head, The Fabulous Freebirds gained national infamy with their grueling feud with the Von Erichs and their passion to prove the superiority of six-man tag team matches. But the World Class fans were less than impressed with these Bad Street party-mongers, and naturally, anyone foolish enough to wage war against their beloved Von Erichs was bound to receive something less than affection from the Texas fans.

Michael Hayes, Terry "Bam Bam" Gordy, and Buddy Roberts wrestled Kerry, Kevin, and Mike Van Erich in a variety of grudge-filled tag team and singles matches, and both camps took turns wearing the World Class Six-Man Tag Team belts. Finally, the Von Erichs' title was upheld by officials over a controversy surrounding the "legal man in the ring" during a title match in Texas Stadium. This was to be expected from the Freebirds, who were employing a brawling, rule-breaking style to combat the Von Erichs' high-flying scientific approach.

To settle the dispute, an awesome match was fought with all six men in the ring at once. Needless to say, it was a wild flurry of action. Hayes squared off with Kerry Von Erich, while Roberts took on Kevin, and "Bam Bam" locked up with the over-matched Mike. Kerry frustrated Hayes with a series of scientific holds, punching when necessary.

Meanwhile, Gordy had dazed Mike with a powerful forearm and was no longer pummeling him with Suplexes, Neck Breakers, and his spleen-splintering Piledriver. Quickly, he covered Mike for a pinfall, but the other Von Erichs, who were fairing better, elbow-smashed Gordy and the match continued. Kerry got Hayes in the Abdominal Stretch and—with the other wrestlers

punching, and gouging in the hopes of victory. The Freebirds were definitely getting the worst of it. Finally, a semi-conscious Michael Hayes fell through the cage's chain-link door. The Von Erichs has won.

It seemed like a good time to move on. The Freebirds next entered their home state of Georgia, where they were welcomed with open arms. "Freebird" by Lynyrd Skynyrd was played over the P.A. as they strutted into the ring and the fans shouted their approval. The Freebirds had come to Georgia to serve notice to the then-hated Road Warriors.

The Road Warriors quickly left

for the AWA, however, under the auspices of a pending NWA ban. The Freebirds' presence was almost anti-climatic. And so, despite their popularity, it was time once again to move on.

While in Georgia, the Freebirds had found time to record a single and video of Hayes' "Bad Street, U.S.A.," and Hayes decided that New York was the place to go. The other Freebirds went along knowing that the move to the Big Apple was supposed to bring Hayes closer to the music industry. Rumors of a Freebird split began to circulate: Did Michael Hayes have stars in his eyes?

But instead of signing up with

a New York record label, Hayes and the Freebirds signed on with the World Wrestling Federation under the management of David Wolff. Wolff was also managing Cyndi Lauper, who was just beginning to establish the so-called "rock 'n' wrestling connection." Perhaps Hayes could have it both ways—a music biz hot shot like Dave Wolff couldn't hurt in the managerial helm. But although Wolff is a brilliant manager of pop stars, this was his first attempt at managing professional wrestlers. Maybe it was Wolff's novice status as a wrestling entrepeneur, or perhaps it was the lack of six-man competition in the WWF. Either

way, the Freebirds found themselves on the road one more time.

Currently they are wrestling as fan favorites, appearing with the Pro Wrestling U.S.A. group. Certainly, they have lost none of their flamboyant ring style. They continue to carry on the Bad Street tradition of partying with friends and Piledriving everyone else.

The Fabulous Freebirds (from left to right): Terry "Bam Bam" Gordy, Michael Hayes, and Buddy Roberts. Not only has this trio revitalized tag team wrestling, but they've also strengthened the "rock 'n' wrestling" connection.

THE IRON SHEIK AND NIKOLAI VOLKOFF

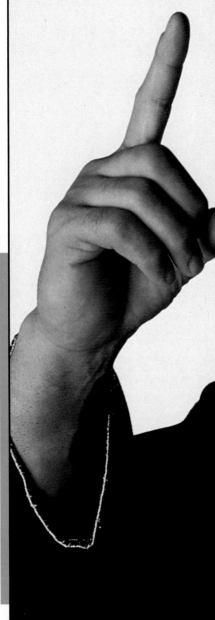

Nikolai Volkoff (left) and the Iron Sheik have turned the wrestling ring into an arena for international politics.

Weight: 605 pounds (combined)
Hometowns: Tehran, Iran/ Moscow, U.S.S.R.
Best Move: Baiting Patriotic Americans
Titles Held: WWF Tag Team Champions

The Iron Sheik and Nikolai Volkoff have already elicited perhaps the greatest rain of contempt from wrestling fans in history. Both are extremely proud of their homelands, and despite overwhelming disapproval from wrestling fans, they continue to flaunt their national pride.

The Iron Sheik's Iranian flag and ritualistic worship of the Ayatollah's image are quick to enrage American audiences, which still remember the Iranian hostage crisis. And the sight of "The Hollywood Fashion Plate" in the guise of Ayatollah Blassie is enough to make even the most cowardly pencil-necked geek want to get drafted. But make no mistake: For all these anti-American carryings on, The Iron Sheik is one of wrestling's greatest competitors.

Formerly a bodyguard for the Shah of Iran, Hussein Vaziri (as he was then known) became a national hero when he won Silver Medals for wrestling in both the '72 Olympics and Pan-American Games. The furious political climate in Iran forced Hussein to denounce the Shah and come to America. With him, he brought his Persian exercise clubs, his infamous pointed-toe boots, and a bank book listing millions in petroleum assets. With his sensational amateur background and large amounts of cash, even the most patriotic promoter could not turn down The Iron Sheik.

Even Bruno Sammartino calls The Iron Sheik the "King of the Suplex," and there is no doubt that it is the Sheik's most devastating legal maneuver. Be it a Vertical Suplex, a Back-to-Belly Suplex, a Double-Underhook Suplex, or the dreaded Iranian "Tehran Terror" Suplex, the effect

The Iron Sheik represented Iran in the '72 Olympics, where he won a medal in wrestling. A former bodyguard of the Shah, he now worships the Ayatollah, and brings his photo into the ring.

Manager Fred Blassie shows off his terrifying team—The Iron Sheik (left) and Volkoff.

is not only demoralizing, it is downright destructive. And when the Sheik brought his rainbow of destruction to New York, it was the end of Bob Backlund's days of glory.

It was the day after Christmas in 1983, and 22,000 fans packed Madison Square Garden to see "The All-American Boy" defend his World Wrestling Federation Title against Iran's Iron Sheik. There was more at stake here than the title. Backlund symbolized everything American—he was clean-cut, morally upright, and most of all, he upheld every tenet of good sportsmanship. On the other hand, the Sheik and his manager Fred Blassie were not only hated rulebreakers, they were anti-Americans as well.

The Garden was at a fever pitch at the two-minute mark. The Sheik, after a moment's frustration from Backlund's Armdrags, had reversed the momentum with a Vertical Suplex and he now held Backlund in a painful Surfboard Hold, his controversial footwear jammed into the small of the Champ's back. Less than ten minutes later, he clamped on the Camel Clutch and Backlund's six-year reign came to an end. The Iron Sheik became the most hated man ever to wear the WWF World Championship belt.

But the dynasty only lasted 28

From left to right: Nikolai Volkoff, the Iron Sheik, and Fred Blassie, "The King of Men." This dastardly, anti-American trio hopes to one day rule the wrestling world.

days. One month later, in the same coveted arena, the Sheik lost the belt to Hulk Hogan, whom promoters had substituted for an injured Backlund. "We didn't train for this tanned geek!" screamed Blassie. No one listened, and Hulk-a-mania was born.

Over the next few months, the Sheik and Blassie had some trouble getting a rematch, and the Sheik got caught up in Sgt. Slaughter's crusade for America. Certainly, there was no better target for Slaughter's frustrations, and the ensuing feud was one of the wildest and bloodiest fans had ever seen, culminating in a "Texas Deathstyle Boot Camp Match" in Madison Square Garden. It was about this time that Blassie brought in the awesome Nikolai Volkoff.

The barrel-chested Russian was no stranger to the WWF—Blassie had managed him several years before and even got him a title match against Backlund. But now more than ever, Volkoff would be an intimidating asset in Blassie's stable. The Sheik and Volkoff began training together immediately. Aligning their anti-American philosophies with brutal ring savvy, they became a lethally efficient combination. The Iron Sheik's arsenal of Suplexes and scientific technique (not to mention his infamous boots) coupled with Volkoff's incredible stature and his crippling Russian Backbreaker became the basis for what Blassie calls the greatest tag team of all time. Certainly they are the most hated—the Sheik's antics and Volkoff's insistence on singing the Soviet national anthem

(in a rather pleasing baritone) never fails to have the audience throwing debris into the ring. And with the flag-waving "American Express" team of Windham and Rotundo as champs, it was clearly time for the Sheik and Volkoff to make their bid for the gold. At the historic WrestleMania card, they got it.

Madison Square Garden was packed. Another million were watching on closed circuit TV. Once again, the pride of America was at stake as "The American Express," managed by the infamous Captain Lou Albano, defended their WWF Tag Team Title against The Iron Sheik and Nikolai Volkoff.

It began as a scientific match with the Sheik and Mike Rotundo trading Suplexes and Arm Locks. Then Volkoff tagged in and crunched Rotundo with a devastating Backbreaker. The Russian continued to pummel his opponent with Body Slams, ramming him head first into The Iron Sheik's eagerly waiting boot.

The beaten Rotundo managed to tag out and a fresh Barry Windham charged into the ring. Quickly, he set up Volkoff for his pet move, the Bulldog. But a quick-thinking Fred Blassie handed the Sheik his cane and instructed him to use it. The referee's back was turned when the cane came wailing down on Windham's skull. He hit the mat and Volkoff covered him for an easy pin. Captain Lou's ranting and raving didn't help a bit. Blassie, The Iron Sheik, and Nikolai Volkoff, three of the sport's greats, came out of the match victorious.

THE ROAD WARRIORS: HAWK AND ANIMAL

Weight: 565 pounds
(combined)
Hometown: Chicago, Illinois
Best Move: The Double Piledriver
Titles Held: National Tag Team
Champions, World Tag Team
Champions

They all use theme songs nowadays. It's gotten so a main eventer can't stalk down the aisle without some hoary anthem pacing his footsteps. Most of them don't make any sense. Manny Fernandez using "Beat It"? The Hi-Flyers prancing around to the tune of Bruce Springsteen's "Badlands"?

But Black Sabbath's "Iron Man" is the perfect music to wrestle to. The opening chord ripples up the fans' spines as huge painted predators of class and distinction stride into the ring. There is nothing more exciting in wrestling than the Legion of Doom climbing through the ropes.

In fact, the Road Warriors are almost too exciting for their own good. The wholly spontaneous standing ovations they receive are somewhat bewildering to promoters and other traditionalists. The old fan favorite/rulebreaker standard doesn't apply here. The Warriors specialize in brutality, and yet the fans are cheering. What's going on here?

Yes, the Road Warriors are sadistic. No, they don't care whether they cripple and/or hospitalize their opponents. Yes, they break the rules. But wrestling is a sport for sadists who like to hurt people and break rules.

Like any other hard contact sport, wrestling is institutionalized barbarism, a sport in which the infliction of pain is a prerequisite to victory. In boxing, the noble art of self-defense, the point of the game is to knock your opponent into unconsciousness. In wrestling, the objective is to gain a pinfall or submission, which means you either hurt your opponent or cut off the blood supply to his brain until he passes into a faint.

The fans cheer the Road Warriors because they hurt people with maximum efficiency. When Hulk Hogan gouges Roddy Piper's eyes, the fans cheer; why not cheer a bone-crushing Belly-to-Belly Suplex, or five consecutive Backbreakers, or a punch in the kidneys?

In fact, the Road Warriors' enormous support may be signaling a new objectivity among the mass of fans. The Road Warriors are wrestlers, and that's still more important to them than their image. If Hawk and Animal started wearing tutus tomorrow, they'd still have the raw skill and double-tough instinct to pound their hapless adversaries into the sour-smelling canvas.

But they'd never wear tutus. They grew up on the streets. Chicago has always been a city of extremely well-organized youth gangs, and Hawk and Animal led one of the fiercest. They grew up on AWA TV broadcasts, idolizing immortals like the Bruiser, The Crusher, and Fritz Von Erich. (Such is their admiration of The Crusher that they concentrated their offensive on Baron Von Raschke during their AWA title matches with the two.) They utilized wrestling skill in rumbles, Suplexing while armed with chains and proving to others that a Piledrive on a cracked urban parking lot is deadlier than a tire iron. Wary of the state pen and uninterested in hustling for the rest of their lives, they decided to take up their first love as a legitimate career.

Animal had been wrestling in prelims for about nine months and was training with Hawk when a husky, verbose man in a yellow hat started haunting their gym workouts. Hawk and Animal, unaware of his background, took notice of his taking notice. Hawk beckoned him into the ring with one meaty finger. "If you want me to beat the crap out of you, sissy boy, step inside," Hawk yelled. Three Corkscrew Neckbreakers later, Hawk looked up at Precious Paul Ellering and knew that he and Animal had found a manager.

Ellering took them into his Legion of Doom and they stomped over all opposition in Georgia. The National Tag Team Belts were theirs for the asking. Fans and insiders were overwhelmed. The Warriors were voted "Tag Team of the Year" in a 1983 *Pro Wrestling Magazine* readers' poll, an amazing accomplishment considering it was their first full year of competition.

Relations with Ellering became increasingly strained, however. Ellering is a fine manager, but he tends to be too manipulative. Although he was instrumental in refining their natural ability, Ellering was a better financial manager than a wrestling coach. Ellering is not the brilliant teacher and strategist along the lines of J.J. Dillon and Lou Albano; the best he has done for Hawk and Animal was to secure a contract with *World Championship Wrestling* when they had no connections in the biz. Tired of being underpaid bounty hunters on the trail of men Ellering hated, like the Sawyer brothers and Jimmy Valiant, the Warriors not only fired him but also cracked his arm like a breadstick to teach him a lesson. Ellering came crawling back soon after his limb was set, brandishing a much more lucrative contract in his good hand. (He would have been finished as a manager without Hawk and Animal; over a six-month period, Buzz Sawyer, the Iron Sheik, and King Kong Bundy all walked out on him for different reasons.)

Faced with paltry competition, however, the Warriors grew stale. After a shocking upset loss to Ronnie Garvin and Jerry Oates, Hawk and Animal packed their bags for the AWA, where they won the World Tag Team Title in less than six weeks. They have not encountered a serious threat to their title reign since.

Arguably, the Road Warriors are the pre-eminent story in wrestling today. Roddy Piper, Hulk Hogan, Sgt. Slaughter, Ric Flair, the Von Erichs, and Vince McMahon, Jr., have all transfigured wrestling history in recent years. But the Road Warriors' popularity and influence are unprecedented. Grizzled experts already tout them as the greatest tag team in history, and they are also more popular than other grapplers in the AWA.

Hawk and Animal still have their critics. Some conservative members of the NWA Board of Governors initiated a move to ban them when they were National Champions for "excessive brutality" and "negative role modeling." The motion was not

The Animal demonstrates his Neckbreaker on a hapless opponent.

only ridiculously vague in its wording but clearly unconstitutional, and it was quickly dropped. Others complain that the Warriors don't know how to wrestle. "All they do is kick and punch," complained one correspondent for a national magazine. *Au contraire!!!* Hawk and Animal possess exceptional scientific knowledge. They concentrate on power moves, for obvious reasons, but they are ferocious artisans of power. No one, not even the Iron Sheik or Magnum T.A., can execute a Belly-to-Belly Suplex better than Hawk. Both Hawk and Animal can decapitate geeks with a Clothes-line comparable to Stan Hansen's or the Masked Superstar's, and there is *no* defense for their Double Piledriver outside of staying in the dressing room.

Will success and the fans' adulation ruin the Road Warriors? Can they maintain their sadistic fire in the cool breeze of the cheers? Will they constantly adapt their wrestling style to keep their opponents off-guard, as all champions must, or fall into a rut because their present strategies are so effective? Can Ellering last as their manager? And how will aging affect the proud cannibals, whose pecs and pops have to congeal into fatty tissue as the years advance?

As Hawk and Animal say, "WE DON'T CARE!!!" The Warriors are in charge, and they'll tally their body count.

The excessively brutal Road Warriors, Hawk (left) and Animal joke around (ha, ha) with their manager, Paul Ellering.

THE WONDER WOMEN

Women's wrestling has never been more popular than it is today. Much of the credit for its newfound popularity can be traced directly to rock sensation Cyndi Lauper. When Lauper decided to manage Wendi Richter, it opened up the sport to a whole new legion of fans. But women's wrestling has been around for as long as anyone can remember. The Fabulous Moolah is proof positive of this fact.

For 28 years, Moolah reigned supreme on the women's circuit before she was upset by Wendi Richter in Madison Square Garden. When Moolah was defeated by Richter, it signaled the dawning of a new age in women's wrestling.

Right now, there are several top women wrestlers in the country. The number one contender for Wendi Richter's crown is former champion Lelani Kai. The Hawaiian-born Kai held the women's championship for two weeks before losing it to Wendi. Another top contender on the circuit is U.S. Champion Judy Martin. Judy has been wrestling for eight years and is one of the toughest women around. Beautiful Desiree Petersen is another star to watch. Desiree has the moves it takes to make it all the way to the top. Currently, Desiree and Canadian Velvet McIntyre hold the Women's U.S. Tag Team Title. Absolutely sensational inside the ring, these two lovely ladies have a thorough knowledge of the sport, and should be top wrestlers for a very long time.

Other women stars who bear watching are Peggy Patterson, Candi Devine, Nature Girl, Carol Summers, Debbie Combs, and Susan Green. At any given moment, one of these wonder women could conceivably knock Wendi Richter out of the number one position.

Right: Judy Martin has Desiree Peterson in a strong Chin Lock. Below: Velvet McIntyre. She holds the U.S. Tag Team Championship with Peterson.

Desiree Peterson started her wrestling career in Europe, and is now a big international star.

LELANI KAI

seconds Wendi Richter and Cyndi Lauper made their grand entry. After a verbal shouting match between Moolah and Cyndi Lauper, the bout was underway. Wendi controlled the first few minutes of the battle with her superior skill. Soon Lelani rebounded. Kai, stealing a page from the Fabulous Moolah's book, began to rack her fingers across the champ's eye. Wendi was down. But the champ still had some fight left in her and came back with a solid right forearm, felling the challenger. At this point, the Fabulous Moolah attacked Cyndi Lauper outside the ring. When Wendi saw Moolah choking Cyndi, she ran to her aid. But Moolah quickly clobbered Wendi, sending her sprawling to the mat. Lelani, sensing an easy victory, jumped on Wendi. At the count of three, Lelani Kai was the new Women's World champion.

But Lelani's reign, however, was short lived. On March 31 at the big WrestleMania extravaganza, Richter regained the World's title when she pinned Lelani Kai in center ring.

It's obvious that we have not seen the last of Lelani Kai. The Hawaiian is one tough, determined female and she will be back. It's inevitable. Wendi Richter's reign will never be secure as long as talented women like Lelani Kai are waiting in the wings.

With the help of her coach, the Fabulous Moolah, Lelani Kai won the Women's World Wrestling Championship from Cyndi Lauper's protégé Wendi Richter on March 17, 1985. Unfortunately for Kai, Richter reclaimed the title in a rematch held just two weeks later.

Weight: 138 pounds
Hometown: Honolulu, Hawaii
Best Move: Defeating Wendi Richter
Titles Held: Women's World Champion

Hawaiian born Lelani Kai has always followed in the footsteps of the Fabulous Moolah.

Lelani learned the ropes in a training camp run by the fabulous one. After watching Kai in action, it's obvious that she has a thorough knowledge of the various scientific holds and aerial maneuvers, plus a liberal sprinkling of Moolah's illegal tricks interspersed in her repetoire.

Lelani's approach to the sport was also influenced by the teachings of her uncle, Professor Toru Tanaka. "If it weren't for my uncle, I wouldn't be in this position today," Lelani admitted.

"I always wanted to be a wrestler but when I told my uncle, he tried to discourage me. Finally, he said that if I was still interested in becoming a wrestler when I turned 18, he would introduce me to Moolah. True to his word, he did, and that's why I'm here today."

During her initial training, Lelani was put through five hours of grueling workouts a day consisting of calisthenics, tumbling, and running, plus workouts on the mat. After six months of sheer torture, Lelani made her debut in California against Susan Green. In her first match, the Hawaiian didn't do as well as she had hoped, but she proved that she learned her lessons well. That was ten years ago. In the ensuing years Lelani worked very hard trying to master her trade. Many times in the past Moolah stated, "Lelani is definitely

going to be one of the top women wrestlers in the sport. I've seen quite a few girls come into the sport and I've trained quite a few myself but I've never seen anyone with quite the determination and ring savvy that Lelani possesses. She is definitely future championship material."

The Fabulous One's prognostication was right on the money! After the Fabulous Moolah lost the Women's World Title to Wendi Richter, Moolah went out and worked with Lelani Kai. Moolah refined Lelani's skills in hopes that she would be able to defeat Wendi Richter and win the Women's World Title.

On March 17, 1985, Madison Square Garden was packed to the rafters. Lelani Kai, accompanied by the Fabulous Moolah, was the first participant in the ring. Soon "Girls Just Want to Have Fun" blared over the loud speakers. In

THE FABULOUS MOOLAH

Weight: 138 pounds
Hometown: Columbia, South Carolina
Best Move: Holding the Title for 28 Years
Titles Held: Woman's World Champion

The Fabulous Moolah is a living legend. No other wrestler in the sport has ever held a championship as long as the Fabulous One—not Ric Flair, Rick Martel, or Hulk Hogan of the current generation, nor Bruno Sammartino, Lou Thesz, Buddy Rogers, or Strangler Lewis from the last one. No one has ever come close to lasting 28 years as champion.

The Fabulous Moolah began her professional career in 1954. At first, she served as a "slave girl" for a wrestler who went under the name "The Elephant Boy." But Moolah longed to be in the spotlight all by herself. When the big break finally came her way, Moolah was ready. In 1956 Moolah entered a tournament to crown a new Women's World Champion. Moolah easily progressed to the finals where she was matched against former champion June Byers. The Fabulous Moolah emerged triumphant.

For the next 28 years, the queen easily knocked off every heir to the throne. Kitty Adams, Peggy Patterson, Donna Christinello, Toni Rose, Jayne Grable, Paula Kaye, Vicki Williams, Vivian St. John, Suzette Ferrara, and numerous others tried their best against the queen, but no one even came close to pinning Moolah's shoulders to the mat. That is until July of 1984.

Madison Square Garden was filled to capacity while millions more waited patiently to see "The War to Settle the Score" on MTV. Moolah was being challenged by tough Texan Wendi Richter. If anyone knew Moolah it was Richter. Wendi had been trained by the Moolah and had observed the queen in action many times. Wendi had something else going for her as well—the backing of rock sensation Cyndi Lauper and Lauper's numerous fans.

The bout came about in the aftermath of an argument between Lauper and Captain Lou Albano. Lauper, in a moment of anger, challenged the Captain. Albano merely laughed it off. When Lauper persisted and said she would get someone to beat the Captain, Albano countered with the best woman in the business, the Fabulous Moolah. "That no-good, singing ingrate will never find anyone who can beat Moolah," Albano thought. He was wrong.

Lauper immediately hooked up with Wendi Richter. The star proceeded to put Wendi through grueling workout sessions. Then she dressed her up, frizzed her hair, and a star was born. The rest, as they say, is history.

Although the Fabulous Moolah is no longer the queen of the sport, don't count her out so fast. There's still plenty of fight left in the Fabulous One.

The Fabulous Moolah is one of the most famous wrestlers of all time, man or woman. She held the Women's World Championship title for an unprecedented 28 years, and now splits her time between wrestling and coaching.

WENDI
RICHTER

Height: 5'10"
Weight: 140 pounds
Birthplate: Dallas, Texas
Attributes: Women's World Heavyweight Champion, Tag Team Champion

Wendi Richter has reversed the standard routines generally practiced by female sex symbols. As a rule, sex symbols push their physical attractiveness to hype

Wendi Richter's manager, pop star Cyndi Lauper, watches with concern as Wendi fights it out in the ring.

their careers at their outset, and then demand to be taken seriously as artists as they expand the breadth of their work. Wendi, however, began as a grappler with unlimited potential, and *then* shifted gears into supercharged pin-up status.

It is, to some extent, a shame to introduce an article about such a gifted wrestler by discussing the implications of her sex appeal. But it is unavoidable. Wendy Richter *is* beautiful; if anyone deserves the VA VA VA VOOM championship belt in women's

wrestling, it would have to be Richter. She strikes a resonant chord in the heart of each male fan for a deeper reason, though; here's a *tough* woman whose natural eroticism has no bearing on her businesslike wrestling technique. She cares about wrestling more than your basic male fan's wife or girlfriend—and translates into the perfect combo of lover and wrestling fan for the

guy who can't explain wrestling's appeal to a woman. Of course, a hefty percentage of wrestling fans are female, but the sport accentuates a tough guy dialect which often can't penetrate the barriers of culturally conditioned sex roles.

Herein lies the tragedy of Wendi's current sex symbol stance. Instead of impressing wrestling fans as a gorgeous female wrestler thrashing it out in the ring with self-confident fury, Wendi chooses to parade herself as a cutie pie who blows soap

bubbles at the camera and allows gaffers to slather her body with hideous red makeup. Worse yet, she is reinforcing a double standard; if good-looking male grapplers like Roddy Piper and Ken Patera flaunt their physical charms, they get hooted down as sissies.

But to go back to the beginning, Wendi Richter was a natural. Promoters knew she would be a star even before she signed for her first professional match. Her first match happened to be against Vicki Williams, one of the toughest competitors in women's wrestling. Wendi lasted a full 12 minutes before she was pinned. Other female wrestlers were drooling to use her as a tag team partner, and Richter decided to work with Joyce Grable, another superstar of women's wrestling. They quickly annihilated Judy Martin and Richter's future nemesis, Lelani Kai, for the World Tag Team Title. Wendi had ascended to ring glory fast—very fast, like hot mercury. Guess who didn't notice? Everyone in the wrestling establishment. As it still is today, women's wrestling was second class. In the eyes of the media, Wendi's triumph seemed less important than Tommy Rich's biennial dental checkup.

Nonetheless, insiders knew that she could revolutionize women's wrestling. Promoters courted some of the smaller male wrestlers, the Terry Taylors and Hacksaw Sawyers of the sport, to try and arrange a mixed singles

Cyndi Lauper (left) talks to her star during a break in the action. Richter is one of the top women in wrestling today, and promises to be a contender for years to come.

match involving Richter. Unsurprisingly, no man would volunteer to go up against Wendi; imagine their humiliation if a lady beat them senseless! This was more than a distinct possibility—experts still agree that Wendi can easily pin most men of comparable size. She proved she was certainly not physically intimidated by men by beating up a number of referees whose officiating had displeased her.

Along with her startling skill, she had a natural killer instinct. She was acknowledged to be the meanest woman in the mat wars, a cruel competitor with a penchant for keeping the arena stretcher-handlers busy. Many of her opponents developed bad colds and stomach viruses when they knew they were to wrestle the fearsome Richter.

And then one night, Richter returned home after a grueling tour of matches and absent-mindedly turned on the playback of her telephone-answering machine. A squeaky, frazzled-sounding voice with an exaggerated New York accent reverberated through her living room. . . .

Cyndi Lauper needed a mercenary to wage war against the sexist Lou Albano, and she could buy just about any female wrestler she wanted with her record royalties. The only truly wealthy woman in wrestling was the Fabulous Moolah, 27 years a World's Champion. Although Lauper knew practically zilch about wrestling, she had the good sense to ask insiders who the finest woman after Moolah was. The consensus among experts was that a woman named Wendi Richter could *beat* Moolah on a good night, and had come *very* close to doing so on several occasions already.

It looked like a great deal for Wendi. She would have another shot at Moolah, whose age was finally creeping up on her greatness. She would make a ton of money, finally earning a wage commensurate with those of male stars. Hopefully, the match's attendant hype and publicity would bring women's wrestling to

Wendi Richter has a natural killer instinct—she's the meanest woman in the sport. It's not uncommon for a scheduled opponent to feign illness to avoid battling Richter.

the forefront, where it belonged.

Well, Wendi won the match and the title (on a highly controversial pin), and has held it since, excepting the six weeks in which she loaned it to the Moolah-managed Leilani Kai. However, she has backed down from a position of revolutionary influence. Unlike Moolah, who defended her title against all comers, Richter has signed an exclusive contract with the WWF. Though she doesn't wish to degrade her championship, she has opted for a less aggressive style. Richter wrestles brilliantly on occasion, but no longer rolls over opponents like a raging human dynamo. (This happens to many first-time champions who seem awed by their responsibilities; expect her to toughen up in her second reign.) Finally, the bikini poses and scanty wrestling togs she now favors seem to her detractors (especially other female wrestlers) as exploitation of the worst kind. And for whatever reason, women's wrestling is no more visible now than it was when Moolah was champ.

In 1983, Atlanta's Omni hosted a card of matches which included both the Men's and Women's Battle Royal. The winner of the former would win $25,000, while only $10,000 would be awarded to the last woman in the ring during their Battle Royale. When Richter's ex-partner Grable found out about the disparity, she refused to wrestle that night as a personal protest. Will Wendi, with her prestige and influence, take a similar stand in defense of women's wrestling? Moolah herself was instrumental in having New York State's ban on women's wrestling lifted in 1971. Of course, Richter would prefer to keep her mind on wrestling and stay out of politics, but her unique position of influence demands a crusading spirit.

Wendi Richter has the potential to be not only the greatest female wrestler in history, but a catalyst for social change as well. It will be fascinating to see what she does with both.

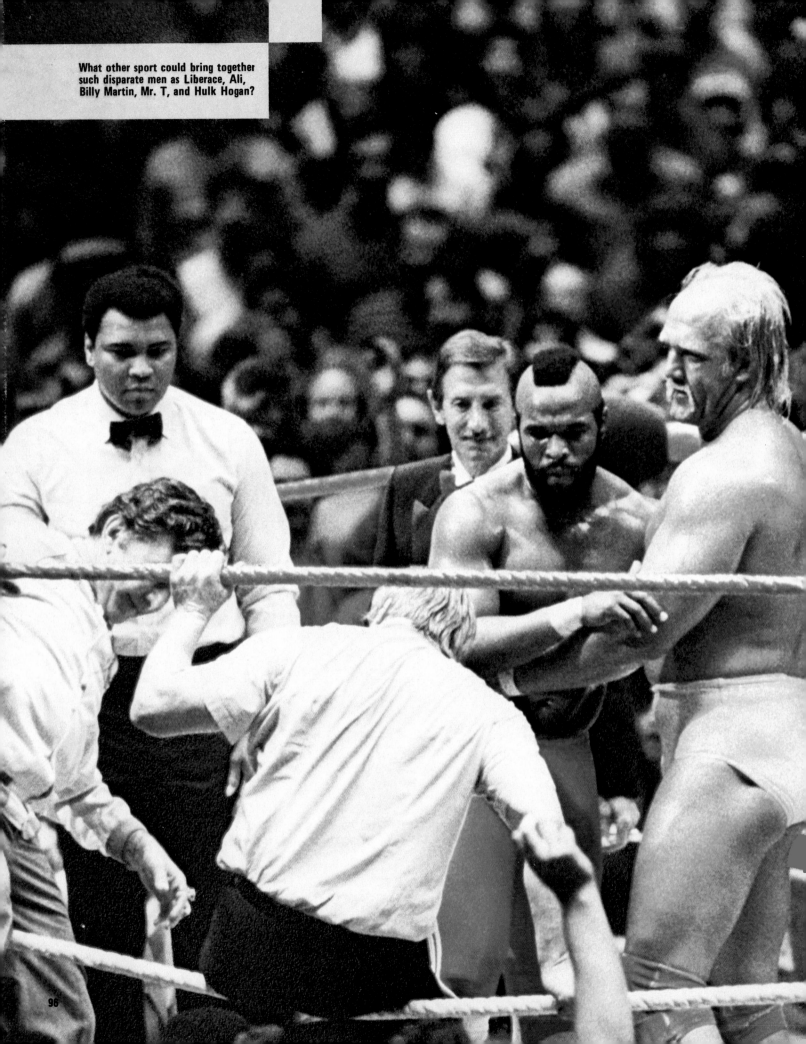

What other sport could bring together such disparate men as Liberace, Ali, Billy Martin, Mr. T, and Hulk Hogan?